BUGGIES AND
BAD TIMES

Third in the series
MEMORIES OF
HOOSIER HOMEMAKERS

Eleanor Arnold
Editor and Project Director

F. Gerald Handfield Jr.
Indiana Historical Society
Oral History Consultant

Paul Wilson
Photographic Consultant

From Hoosier Homemakers Through The Years
an oral history project of
The Indiana Extension Homemakers Association

TABLE OF CONTENTS

PREFACE

The Project

This book is the third in the series, Memories of Hoosier Homemakers, which arises from an ongoing oral history project. This book deals with two of the subjects discussed in the collected interviews. The first is changes in transportation, as observed by the narrators, and the second is the impact of world events on the lives and values of the family.

The first book of the series, *Feeding Our Families,* was about homemakers and food, discussing how women have grown, harvested, preserved, cooked and served food. Other chapters touched on the social implications of food served at home to guests and outside the home at community and social occasions.

The second book, *Party Lines, Pumps and Privies,* dealt with the coming of new technologies in housework and the changes such technology made. Changes in heating, washing, ironing, cleaning, cooling, obtaining water and changes in communication, including memories of telephones, phonographs, radio and television, were discussed.

These three books, a slide/tape program and the other books planned in the series are the outgrowth of an oral history project sponsored by the Indiana Extension Homemakers Association in view of its 75th anniversary in 1988. The project is called Hoosier Homemakers through the Years and was originally planned as an organizational history; however, the scope of the project has been widened to include a study of women in their role as homemakers.

Funded by the Indiana Committee for the Humanities and supported by the parent organization, the project asked volunteers to conduct interviews all over Indiana. To date, interviews have been received from 80 of the 92 counties, so that the project is truly statewide in character.

A crucial factor in the program has been its talented and dedicated volunteer personnel. All interviews were conducted by volunteers, after a day's training by F. Gerald Handfield, Assistant Director, Field Services, Indiana Historical Society. At their own or their county's expense, these volunteers conducted interviews and, in many cases, transcribed them themselves before sending them in to the project. The project director and the oral history committee, volunteers all, have processed and indexed the interviews, which will be available for public use at the end of the project. They will be housed at the Indiana Historical Society Library in Indianapolis.

In addition to the interviews, a collection of visual materials, including photographs, newspaper articles, programs and other such materials was made. Women of the organization brought in large quantities of very good material and it was copied on the spot. This material will also be housed at the Indiana Historical Society, in their photographic collection.

From the visual material and the recorded voices of the women interviewed, a slide/tape program called *Hoosier Homemakers: The Early Years* has been made. This program has been extremely popular, having circulated widely over the state and having had much use in academic, organizational, museum and library audiences. Over 20,000 people are estimated to have seen this program.

An interesting outgrowth of the Indiana project was the initiation of such a project at the national level by the National Extension Homemakers Council, with the Indiana project director acting as director of this project also. The Indiana project now serves as a pilot project for the national project.

Several other states, having become aware of the work from the national project, are now starting similar ambitious projects in their own state organizations, so that the circle has been completed.

Everyone concerned with the project has been extremely gratified by its achievements. The almost complete lack of documentation about the role of homemakers led them to believe that there was a great need for the project, and the fine response to the project has confirmed this belief.

D'Ann Campbell, Indiana University, wrote, "This project makes a long-overdue inquiry into the lives of a major group in our state's population. It is women's history in a distinctive form, in no way ideological, but rather the discovery of a nearly invisible and inarticulate, and surely undocumented, segment of women who are yet one of the main forces in Indiana's society."

Eleanor Arnold
Editor and Project Director
R.R. 2, Box 48
Rushville, IN 46173
317/932-5204

EDITOR'S NOTES

A few notes may aid the reader's understanding of the way this book has been edited. The book is composed entirely, aside from editorial comment, of words taken from the project interviews. My task, as editor, was to select these words and place them in order, so that the experiences of many women could become a coherent whole.

In order to make the sense of the interview clear, I had to omit false starts and repetitions and, in some cases, have had to cut extraneous material for the sake of brevity and coherence. The words, however, are the words they spoke.

Occasional words or phrases will be found in brackets [ ]. Here I have added something to clarify the excerpt or to explain the meaning of a word which might be unfamiliar.

Words in bold type are the words of the person conducting the interview and those in regular type are the words of the narrator. In the back of the book is a list of interviewers and interviewees, listed by counties, so that the interested reader may find who has conducted any interview.

The name following the excerpt is the name of the person who is talking. Her age at the time of the interview and her county are included to help the reader place the era and locale from which her memories came. A map of Indiana inside the back cover shows the location of the counties.

Transcriptions, which were done in the counties, varied somewhat in the use of colloquial spellings [gonna for going to, etc.] and in general we have followed the transcriber's rendition.

Visual material in the book came from materials collected by and from the homemakers, unless otherwise noted. Some photographs are from the collection of J. C. Allen, who was staff photographer at Purdue University for many years and did extensive coverage of extension activities.

INTRODUCTION

The Women and World Events

From pre-history on, the role of homemaker has traditionally belonged to women. The work of keeping house and the less tangible task of maintaining a good family life have long been understood to be women's responsibility. And, whether through nature or nurture, they have accepted the responsibility and have trained themselves for this role.

Women through the ages have worked hard, both physically and emotionally, to maintain a well-provisioned, happy and secure home. They felt they were successful when this goal had been achieved.

Through the ages, individual families have been affected by world events.
Submitted by Daviess County

But security can be threatened from outside sources as well as forces in the home, and usually these outside forces are beyond the control of the homemaker. No amount of floors scrubbed or bedtime stories read can forestall a world war or put back the clock on changing technology.

When major upheavals occur in the nation or in the world, they may cause drastic changes in the home and family. They may alter family life, either temporarily or permanently. They break the orderly continuity.

Therefore, homemakers have a different perspective on history. Although they are fully aware of world events, and judge them wisely and calmly, their true concern is for the changes which these events will bring in their own sphere of concern—the home.

Most history is bad news. Eras are marked by wars or by other drastic financial or social changes. And bad news for the country is usually bad news for the home.

Wars are a time of anguish as husbands, sons and brothers join the armed services. They are gone, and the unspoken possibility of their death is always present. Wars bring rationing and shortages to the home, and increased demands for homemakers to join the work force.

The women interviewed learned to cope. They stood in lines for ration books and traded coupons for things they needed more. They wrote letters to relatives and friends in the armed services and sent packages of candy and cookies overseas. They worked harder at home and/or took on outside jobs to help the war effort. They stayed cheerful and calm and prayed everything would someday return to normal. And, for most, it did.

Times of personal financial crisis may occur at any time, but the Great Depression affected almost everyone. Again, homemakers were deeply concerned by the threat to home and family, as unemployment and low farm prices caused great financial distress.

With little or, in some cases, no financial resources, they learned to cope. They made clothes from feed sacks and from other people's hand-me-downs. They gardened and canned and butchered meat. They sold chickens and eggs and cream and butter they had produced and used the scant cash from the sale for the most pressing financial needs. They learned lessons they never forgot on the necessity of frugal habits. And, eventually, times got better.

World events had threatened the world of these women, but they took direct action to keep their homes together.

During wars, as much as they could, they maintained the unity of the family by writing letters full of day-to-day doings, by sending familiar foods to those far away, and by working hard to maintain the normalcy of the world the soldiers would return to.

During the Depression years homemakers exerted great efforts of resource management and hard work to maintain the way of life they wanted for their family. Food was on the table and the family was clothed. When at all possible, limited resources were shared with extended family members.

The family unit and the family strength were maintained through their efforts. In their understated way, many homemakers will say, after a story of hardships endured, "But we lived through it." Perhaps this says it all. They and their families lived through it as an intact unit.

Their battles are not written in the history books.

BUGGIES AND BAD ROADS

Transportation Through the Years

*"I think when you have gone
from horse and buggy to outer
space travel, you have covered a
good many miles."*

Elizabeth McCullough

The effective size of the world of the homemaker has changed through the years, as modes of transportation have changed.

The day-to-day business and social life of a family takes place in a circle which can be reached in a reasonable time from the home.

For the person who was walking on foot, this might only be a distance of two miles; for the person riding on horseback or in a buggy, it might be five to seven miles.

For the occupant of a Model T auto, an all-day shopping trip to a town twenty miles distant was possible; while the family today may drive or fly thousands of miles to attend a major family event—a wedding or a funeral.

Each step in this process of world widening has been exciting. Memories of the sight of a high-stepping buggy horse, or of the first glimpse of that new invention, the automobile, are remembered with great pleasure. The first ride in a car or in an airplane may have evoked feelings of fear and awe, but the fun was there, too. And now space travel beckons, and that is exciting, also.

Having seen so many changes, the homemakers are ready to believe that still more changes are coming in the future, and that their world will continue to expand.

ON LAND, WITH MUSCLE POWER

Posed humorous picture with two girls
in the buggy shafts.
Submitted by Daviess County

WALKING

Everywhere we went, we walked. Every week we visited my half-sister that didn't live far from us. We visited the neighbors and they visited us. Sometimes we walked miles with the children to visit someone.

Otillia Buehler, 90, Dubois County

We didn't think anything about walkin' two or three miles to a pie supper or a dance or anything. Now they can't walk at all, can they? But that's the only way we had to go.

Grace Hawkins, 93, Martin County

It used to be that we walked a great deal, of course. Now we have lights that we didn't have before. Then, if you went out at night, you took a lantern or just stumbled around in the dark.

Evelyn Buchanan, 78, Scott County

Most of us [young people] walked and met at the schoolhouse and all walked together where we went. Those were happy days—much happier, in my way of thinking, than the children do now. They wouldn't agree with me, but I think so.

Zelma Blocher, 81, Scott County

When I was small, we lived in Munster, which was a small town then. We had no horse or car, so we walked. My grandparents had a horse and buggy, so in bad weather we rode to church with them. In good weather we walked to church and we walked to school.

Mable Hunter, 70, Jasper County

HORSEPOWER

You see, we walked first, and then the preacher came along on horseback.

Alvah Watson, 97, Allen County

Did you ride horseback?
Oh, yes, we all rode horseback.
Bareback?
Yes, more than with a saddle (chuckles).

Lena Alverson, 82, Decatur County

Of course they drove nice horses them days. Everybody had to have a nice horse. My dad never had much.

Thelma Roehr, 69, Posey County

Our horses were more or less pets, of course, and when we, my sister and I, wanted to go anywhere, we'd go take the halter and go to the pasture. We held the halter behind us so that the horse would not see it. And in the other hand we had a nubbin [small ear] of corn. And she [the horse] would see that, she'd come up to eat that nubbin out of our hand, [because] we'd fed her at home many times like that. While she was getting that nubbin, we slipped the halter over her nose and up over her ears, and we had her. And that's the way we caught her to take her up to the barn.

Then we'd have to harness her, feed her, and then we'd get ready and hitch her up to the buggy, and we'd go.

We had about three different horses we could drive, and two of them were workhorses, and they were very slow goers. The other one was more of a driving horse and would travel a little faster, but our folks thought we were safer with one of the workhorses.

Lennie Hern, 90, Decatur County

What kind of a buggy did you have? There were different kinds of buggies, weren't there?

Oh, we had a real nice buggy, a great big buggy, and it was quite foxy. It had side curtains and a fringe around it.

Masa Scheerer, 82, Huntington County

When we went to church, we drove the horse and carriage.

Was that like a buggy?

Well, it [had] two seats instead of one. The carriage was a two-seated vehicle. Father and Mother had a buggy of their own, and we three children had a buggy. The buggy just took one horse, while the carriage took two.

How many people could ride in a carriage?

Six could ride in a carriage, just like six could ride in a two-seated car, you know.

Iva Crouse, 85, White County

I can remember riding in a surrey with the fringe around the top. Mom and Dad had one of those with two seats in it.

That was sort of fancy, wasn't it?

Well, you couldn't hardly get everybody in a buggy, because there was only one seat in it. Then you had to have a surrey, and that had two seats in it.

They used to have lights in the sides. You put little candles in them when you wanted to go out at night, and you lit the candles. They were enclosed with little glasses around them. I can remember riding in it.

Thelma Roehr, 69, Posey County

But for just common going, just one [person] going to town, it was just a buggy. It finally got so we could have a storm apron up in front

A fun ride in a pony cart with a
fringe on top.
Submitted by Blackford County

of the buggy top. And the top would lay back down. In the summer you could fold it up, lay it back in the back, and we had a buggy with a ride in the sunshine.

Lennie Hern, 90, Decatur County

We had a Cozy buggy. It was like a two-seated car, only it was a buggy with two seats, and it was glassed in all around the top, just like your cars are today. You drove a team to it, not one horse. A family with six children [and] a father and a mother, you had to have a little room.

Beulah Grinstead, 68, Hamilton County

Another thing I wanted to tell you about was Grandpa's riding or buggy horses. When he lived in Iowa, he raised racehorses. And he took them around to all the county fairs [and] state fairs. And my dad, when he was just a young man—you know where they hitch the horse to a little cart—well, he would drive the sulky.

Then when they left Iowa he [Grandpa] was out of the racehorse business. But he still kept some of his horses, and he had this one mare that he called Lady. She was coal black, and she was a pacer. She had been a racehorse.

Beautiful horse, I bet.

Oh, she was, and that was his buggy horse. And then he had—I remember that buggy so well—it was just shiny black. And then the wheels and the running gears were bright yellow. Gosh! And Grandpa, he would get out there, with Lady hitched onto that buggy, and he and Grandma would go someplace. And, boy, I thought they really looked like something (chuckles).

Then my dad, he had another old mare called Maude. And she was really old. She was a brood mare that raised these colts, you know. And she was blind. Well, we had old Maude for a time. And when Mother would want to go to town, she would hitch Maude to the buggy. You could hardly get her past a walk, and you had to steer real careful, because she couldn't see where she was going.

So there was a little difference between Lady and Maude?

Oh, my, yes!!

Anna Martin, 79, White County

When I was a girl and went to high school, I had my own horse and buggy. I was the envy of the boys in that school. Dad had bought a horse for me that had been wind-broke. He was a racehorse. Oh, I just raced everything on the road and I had a beautiful time.

Thelma Reedy, 80, Jay County

Was there very much horse racing in this area?

Yes, that was quite a sport in those days. They had a race track over here at Delphi. We had a horse that had been a racer at one time. Dad bought him at a sale. He was a sorrel horse with four white feet. Oh, he was a beautiful animal.

When my brother got old enough to drive, he drove us to school in the horse and buggy [with this horse]. We called him Bill. On the way home from school, sometimes, there would be another horse and

buggy come up in back of us. Well, Bill would just take off and sometimes we'd be going so fast we couldn't make the corner where we were
supposed to turn off at the church. We would just go straight on until
Bill slowed down.

He was a racer, and that stayed with him as long as he lived. Mother
had him after we moved to town. She could go anywhere with Bill.

He was a wonderful horse.

Iva Crouse, 85, White County

One time when Raymond [brother] and I were coming into Burney,
his horse got scared and upset the buggy with us right there in the
street. Fortunately we weren't hurt.

**So you had wrecks in those days, too. Was it a common thing for
horses to run away?**

Well, not really. You'd read about it, and hear about it some, but
not too common.

Lena Alverson, 82, Decatur County

Any accidents that you can recall?

Oh, there was a lot of young kids would take a horse and a buggy
and do a lot of racing with them to see whose horse was the best. Different times they'd get too close and tear the wheels off the buggies.
Just pranks, just as bad as kids are today with their automobiles to see
who can go the fastest.

Masa Scheerer, 82, Huntington County

Tell us about your horses.

Barney was my favorite horse, but he always ran whenever I drove
him. My dad would lead him because he didn't know whether he could
trust me with him. When I would untie him, he wouldn't wait for me
to get into the buggy. He would start right out, and that wouldn't work
very good.

So then I got Frank, and whenever he would be running and he
would see a piece of white paper on the side of the road, he would
jump aside or just shy away from it. He couldn't see very good.

So then I got a mule. I was going to confirmation and I had the
mule in front of the buggy. And when I started out, he went pretty
good, but about a mile down the road, by Ed Otting's gate, he balked
and just stood there.

I got out of the buggy and put a piece of dirt in his mouth. I thought
that would make him forget, but it didn't. He just kept on balking. Ed
Otting saw what was happening, and he came, but he couldn't make
him go either, so he unhitched him. He went home and got me his

white horse, and put him in front of my buggy. And was I ever proud
to drive to confirmation with a white horse.

Hilda Thomas, 83, Jackson County

What did you do when you were courting, compared to kids today?

Well, [we used] a horse and buggy, of course. He bought a buggy for
that special purpose. He hadn't had one before. The horse that he
drove was so used to the road between my place and his that if we
went somewhere and came back and it was late, he would just curl up

Courting couple in buggy enjoy the sun,
with the top folded back.
Submitted by Parke County

in the seat and the horse would go home. He didn't need to drive, he'd
get home (chuckles).

Neva Schlatter, 79, Pulaski County

Our dad bought us a pony when we were kids. We had a cart with it.
We didn't drive it much in the wintertime, but in the summertime we
sure did. We were the only ones in St. Phillips that had a pony.

She was a mean little pony. We used to go to Grandma's through
the woods, and she couldn't wait until someone opened the gate to get
through. Dad had his stock in there, and I would get out and my sister

would say, "I'll stay in the buggy." But before you got the gate open, she [pony] was pawing at you already. She was a mischievous pony. Everybody said ponies aren't mean, but they don't need to tell me that. I know better!!

Did you use your pony just for pleasure?

Right. We used to go different places around just to take the pony and go. We didn't want to walk. But we had to go down to the barn and get her out [or] get her out of the pasture and hitch her up—harness her up.

We had a top on the cart, like a surrey. It had a fringe around the outside of it. It was painted yellow. It was very pretty. We were really fortunate that we had the pony. Not everybody did.

Thelma Roehr, 69, Posey County

And I had a pony, that was very important. And I look back, when I was four years old and one of my boy cousins was three, Georgeanna Harden had a birthday party and that was two miles over the way, and I rode my pony, with him behind me, to that birthday party.

Oh, my, when you were four?

And Mr. Harden tied the pony up and then when we were ready to come home, he set us back on and naturally the pony came home. That pony came home lots of times without me from places.

I don't think I would let my children ride on their pony too far away now.

Well, after all, there weren't any cars. The doctor had a car and that was the only car there was, anywhere near around here.

Beulah Mardis, 76, Johnson County

Later on, we had a driving horse that we'd go down and drive her in the river to wash our buggy.

Did you have to wash the buggy?

Oh, yes, we had to wash the buggy—have it all washed up.

Mary Wolf, 88, Huntington County

In those days the parents had to get the doctor and bring him out to the house and take him home after the baby was born. I remember when one of my little brothers was born that my father did that.

Did your father have a car?

Oh, no, not in those days. He took the horse and buggy and went and got the doctor and took him home.

Agnes Bell, 85, Hamilton County

Some people might not know what a livery stable is for.

Well, a livery stable is a place where you brought your horse and left it during the day. These boys, if they were going to Greensburg, they would drive in from the country and put their horse in the livery stable and take the train to Greensburg or Columbus.

Did they keep them [horses] more than a day?

Oh, yes, if you were going to be gone a week or so, they'd keep it until you came back. And they also had two or three horses that, if you needed to rent a horse, they'd rent them, just like cars, for a short time.

Lena Alverson, 82, Decatur County

Gwins had a livery stable here in town, and they had what they called the pallbearer wagon. They had one wagon for the coffin, the casket, and the next one would be the one the pallbearers rode in [from the church to the cemetery]. It had seats on the side.

And Pop used to rent that wagon from Gwins and hitch up the horses and take all of us kids and Aunt Annie and Uncle Eddie and their family and Uncle Hen and their family. We would go out, and we would take food with us and spend the day, and that was the nicest time.

Mary Flispart, 81, Floyd County

The blacksmith shop was something really necessary, because all the horses had to wear shoes, if they were used off the farm after they had gravel roads. In the wintertime they had to have their horses what they called "roughshod." It was a shoe that was rough on the bottom. A horseshoe that kept them from slipping on the ice.

Virgie Bowers, 81, Pulaski County

My father was a rural mail carrier for fourteen years. He carried the mail with a horse. They called them a mail wagon, something on the order of a horse and buggy. He kept two horses and alternated them.

He had some pretty rough times in the winter sometimes. Once his horse went through the ice on a creek and almost froze before they got it out.

Did they have rural mail boxes?

Yes, they had mail boxes, and at that time people visited with their mail carriers. My father had some very good friends on his mail route. They were so kind to him. When people butchered, they gave him fresh meat, and he had fruit. When the weather was bad, some of the people would bring out coffee and cookies to him. People don't think about that anymore.

Maud Sloneker, 90, Fayette County

Our mailman, when I was small, used to stop and feed his horse up here on the corner. There was a great big post and it had a feed box on top of the post. He would stop and eat his lunch and give his horse a bunch of oats and water him at the schoolhouse pump. Then he would hitch up and go on.

He had one of these little wagons with a top on it, it was like a box on wheels. A regular mail wagon, I guess it was called.

His name was Mr. Pennington. I can remember him. I always thought when I was small—I would tell my mother that Mr. Pennington would make a good Santa Claus, because he was roly-poly. I can remember him plainly.

Ada Clarkson, 70, Jennings County

The mail came by train and it was thrown off. We girls would go to the depot and would pick up the sacks when they threw them off and take them to the post office. We did that to help my husband out, but of course we weren't married then. My brother also worked at the telegraph office, and so we would carry the mail to the post office a lot of the time.

Edna Vandenbark, 92, Howard County

[Longtime small-town postmistress speaking] When I first had the office, I had two carriers with a horse and buggy and what they called mail rigs. They'd have two teams, because the roads were so bad, and they'd have to let one team rest and put the other team on. Now, with improved roads and cars, one carrier takes all that mail.

I remember one of the carriers on a cold winter's day—it was almost dark when he came in. He was just a-laughing when he came in, and he said, "I got something funny to tell you." And with that he slammed down on the table about a thirty-pound ham, smoked, with just the string like they used to [hang them] to smoke them.

He said a lady out here by the Leistner Church was a-standing all wrapped up [waiting for him] and she had that ham. And he said, "I can't take that, you'll have to wrap it." She wanted to send it to her daughter in Louisville. And she said, "Oh, yes, you take that. Eldo Bell [postmistress] will wrap that up and she'll take that. You tell her that I'll pay for it the first time I come to town and bring my eggs." I though that was such a funny thing. There were just things like that they would do.

Eldo Bell, 86, Spencer County

A lot of people went by horse and wagon to take their family. They didn't go to a [bigger] town like Rockville, maybe twice a year. They took their family on the Fourth of July and tax-paying time.

Clyde Smith, 92, Parke County

Now you lived out in the country, quite a little ways from town. Where did you go for your shopping? Where did you buy your groceries?

Out at Kingman. It was about, oh, I'd say about seven miles.

How frequently did you do that?

Once a week.

Was that a special occasion?

It really was. You bought enough groceries at one time to last you all week. You didn't run into town every day to get something.

Laura Drake, 72, Parke County

A pleasant ride in a sleigh with
both well bundled.
Submitted by Rush County

We had a buggy and we drove eight miles. We come to town on Saturday, that was the day to go to town. It would take about an hour to get there and an hour to get home, to drive about eight miles.

Icil Hughes, 78, Grant County

Our shopping was done right in the little towns where we lived, our grocery shopping. If we got to Kokomo, that's where we would buy our clothing. I've driven to Kokomo, a distance of 10 to 12 miles, many a time with my father, in a wagon.

We'd come to town to spend the day; eat cheese and crackers on the courthouse curbing. I don't know whether they had restaurants, anyway we didn't go there. We had cheese and crakers on the courthouse curb.

Edna Vandenbark, 92, Howard County

I know my mother had a brother that lived at Santa Fe and we would start out early on Sunday morning to go down there and visit them, then have dinner and turn around and come back. Fourteen miles down and fourteen miles back. In a horse and carriage, you didn't go too far.

Helen Shockey, 80, Grant County

When you're accustomed to going distances, it doesn't seem to be so far. Four or five miles, in a car, *isn't* far. But four or five miles in a buggy—especially if it's cold—

Neva Schlatter, 79, Pulaski County

What did you do in the wintertime about staying warm?
Well, of course we bundled up pretty good and we had horse blankets for the horses when they were tied to the hitching rack. When we took the blankets off the horse, we'd cover up with the blankets while they were still warm.
What did you do about your feet?
Well, in cold weather Mother would heat several bricks—each one of us had a brick. She would heat that in the oven of the cookstove and would wrap it in several thicknesses of newspaper. We each had one brick to put our feet on. But when we would come back from a place, why we didn't always have warm bricks.

Iva Crouse, 85, White County

One time my mother heated a rock for me to take to keep my hands warm, and a neighbor—they was two girls—she kept on saying, "Oh, Helen's fingers are cold; Helen's hands are cold," till finally I gave her my warm rock and I have always resented it.
She cheated you out of your rock!!

Lois Wagoner, 76, Fulton County

One time, coming home, we had a load of feed in the front of the buggy and each one of us swung a foot out to make room for the feed. And we each frosted one foot coming home. It was cold—we didn't realize it.

Neva Schlatter, 79, Pulaski County

SLEIGHS AND SLEDS

There were times when the snow would get so deep we couldn't drive. They had the big old sleds that they put the wagon bed on. It was a homemade affair, because they would go and get saplings [very small trees] and make runners, and then they would put a wagon bed on it. They hitched the workhorses to it and put straw in the bottom of it, and that's the way we went to school.

And for the buggy, they took the wheels off and put runners on it, and we had a sleigh.

Ruth Dye, 75, Martin County

Neighbors work together to clear the roads of snow.
Submitted by Owen County

We had plenty of snow in them days. 'Course, we traveled quite a bit with horse and sleigh. And seems like the winters were so cold that you could hear the telephone wires sing, which you don't hear anymore. I don't know why. I don't know whether it's the air that has [changed], but in the country you could hear them sing when you would be out in the sleigh.

Mary Ash, 84, Shelby County

Oh, we had snowdrifts, but as long as we had horse-drawn vehicles, we never had problems like we do now. If Dad needed to get the bobsled out to go someplace, he would just hitch the team to the bobsled, and away we went.

Alice Guyer, 68, Wabash County

When we went in the wintertime, we had a bobsled that my father made. That was a wagon bed set on two sets of runners. Two horses were driven to that. One would have a set of sleigh bells on it.

He would put about a foot of straw in the bottom of this wagon bed. The horse blankets would go over that, and we would sit on it with all our wraps and everything on.

When we got to our destination, why the horse blankets went on the horses. In the wintertime, we had our bricks, our warm bricks, to go to visit relatives and to meetings and the like.

Iva Crouse, 85, White County

I was thinking how different it was going to church in those days. Now we go in cars and are home in no time at all. But then you had to get up early and have things organized for the day.

And in wintertime they went by bobsled. Remember the straw and blankets in the bobsleds? I can remember we had a hitching post in front of our church, and the horses were tied there and a feed bag was hung so the horse could eat while we were in church. And the horses were covered with blankets when it was cold.

Margaret Larson, Porter County

I was born in Daviess County on January 15, 1917. It was a very cold day and they told me they had a real big snow and the doctor came in his [bob] sled over to the house.

Verona Lemmon, 65, Daviess County

Do you remember going in a bobsled?

Oh, yes, lots of times. We would go visiting different ones in the family in the wintertime. I don't think they have the snow like they used to, because in wintertime it would be so cold and so much snow, and we would want to go to town. So, instead of going a mile west and then about a mile and a half south, we could—the snow would be over the top of the fences—we would start and go right catty-cornered just across the field.

Then when it would thaw out, it would be a terrible mess. You would get stuck and you couldn't go that way. You would have to go on the road, and then you would hardly get there.

Yes, we went in the bobsled a good many times. At Christmas time, they would have a big Christmas tree out in the middle of the street. Then, in what they called the opera house, they would have a program and treats for the kids. And that would be in the evening, and we'd all go in the bobsled.

Mother would heat the flatirons, and we had what they called soapstone. You would get that hot and put that in. Put straw in the bobsled and some old quilts, and those heated-up things [irons and soapstone] and some blankets and things to put on top of us.

And then Dad would stand up in front and drive the team. And he had a big fur coat that he always wore, and a fur cap. The fur coat was made out of a cow hide, from a steer he had butchered, and sent away and had a coat made out of it. It came clear to his ankles.

Anna Martin, 79, White County

ROADS

Farmers mostly plowed the roads [for snow removal] with horse-power and homemade plows. It was a slow process.

Mable Hunter, 70, Jackson County

I have thought often that we had deeper snows than we do now, because of the types of fences we had. Where there were rail fences there were generally a lot of snowdrifts.

My father was the road supervisor in our area. He made a pointed snowplow and he hitched several horses to that and would open up the roads for ourselves and the neighbors to go to school, or to town, or to church and the like.

Iva Crouse, 85, White County

You know, when I was a child, to me the world was only seven miles big. That was as far as it was to my grandfather's house, and it's just about as far as it was to Marion, the place where we'd get our food. And it'd take all day to make the trip and we'd have to start early. The roads were so bad.

How far was it to Marion?

Nine miles. After roads got pretty good, we could make it in two hours with horses.

Alvah Watson, 97, Allen County

My friend, Rosie Taylor, and I—we'd go over to the schoolhouse to the big programs they would have and some of the boys would ask to bring us home. One night it was raining like crazy, and some of the boys asked to bring us home. We said, gee, that will be nice, we'll accept those dates. We can ride home and not have to walk home through the mud.

The old horses would get scared and, my land, they'd run like crazy and the mud would just fly. They didn't have no side curtains on and the mud would fly over us. When [we] got home, we wished we had walked home. It would have been better than that.

Masa Scheerer, 82, Huntington County

We lived six miles out in the country and had mud roads. When I was in the first grade, my brother and cousin and I drove a team of horses on a two-seat buggy and picked up the neighbor kids to drive to school every day. 'Course, we plodded through a lot of mud, too.

When I was in the fourth and fifth grades and then clear through high school I had to live away from home. I'd go home on weekends; [because of those roads].

Marianne Chamberlain, 54, Newton County

I always went with my husband around the community to things. Sometimes we had to ride a horse out to the car.

Catherine Summers, 67, Harrison County

We had our first car in 1915, and we had a car all the time, but it was usually put up soon after Christmas. Those gravel roads just didn't hold up. I remember going to Greensburg late in January, and we almost didn't get to Clarksburg.

When you planned to go somewhere it was an all-day trip, wasn't it?

Yes. We didn't do it often in those days. We would go into Indianapolis, I can remember, and you had to choose your roads. They weren't all gravel roads.

Mabel Bobbitt, 88, Shelby County

Bourke lived eight miles east of Scottsburg, and I lived five miles west of Scottsburg, so that was thirteen miles. When we first started dating, his daddy had a car. When the roads were not too bad, he would drive the car and come down.

But through the winter, the roads were always too bad. You had to drive horses in winter, because we had mud roads. What wasn't mud was gravel, but in the wintertime when it was bad, you just couldn't drive a car.

Sometimes he would drive the car down and get as far as town, and then he would stop at the livery stable and leave the car and get a horse and buggy and drive the rest of the way in the buggy. Sometimes the weather would be too bad, and he couldn't even get there.

Zelma Blocher, 81, Scott County

We had a lot of plain mud roads. Lot of times, if we did have a gravel road within a half mile of the house, we parked the car at the end of the gravel road and walked up the muddy road.

Alma Small, 61, Dubois County

The roads were so bad at that time that in front of the home owned by Richard and Mary Voland, Leo Richards and Earl Bond were both there with teams of horses to pull out cars who stuck in the mud.

Murriel Sisson, 75, Brown County

What is State Road 3 now was a muddy lane when I was a girl. It used to be hub deep in mud in the wintertime. And my father said one time that some day there would be a pike go through. It wasn't a state road then, it was just called a pike.

I don't know what he would think today if he knew that a state road went by our house.

Irene Redington, 79, Decatur County

For dirt roads they let you work out your road tax. You'd take your team, and sometimes you'd pull that road grader, and sometimes you'd use the scoop. My dad, he had to work that out until he was 60 years old. After you were sixty years old, you didn't have to pay any road tax, if I remember.

But every year you did a certain amount of work to keep up the roads instead of having a county highway department as we have today?

That's right.

Pearl McCall, 89, Daviess County

And a lot of the men, they didn't have money to pay their taxes, and they would do hauling of gravel on the road. They would go along a-raking the roads and they'd give them part of those great big stones that was hauled up and then they'd put them in big mud holes to fill up and then pile in on the others.

Masa Scheerer, 82, Huntington County

I remember when the first highway came through Leopold Township. They rocked it with boulders that they had to pound.

I really have forgotten for sure just when it was opened, but I know in 1926 when my father passed away, the workers had to quit working right below our house so they could get by with the hearse.

Do you remember how they moved their dirt?

Oh, yes, that was done by four-horse teams and scoop shovels and several men of the community were hired to remove the dirt—by hand—a lot was handwork and teamwork. And I think it was for $2.25 a day. A far cry from the way it is moved today.

Mary Gleason, 87, Perry County

They were building gravel roads. We only had mud roads. In the summertime they would have to grade the ditches out and haul other gravel in so we could go home in the wintertime. If they didn't the ditches would go shut and the gravel would go in the ditches, and we would have no road to travel on.

This grading you were talking about, was that done with a mule, or with a team . . .?

Horses, maybe four horses in front of the grader, and there would be a man on there that would turn the wheel, like a steering wheel, and he would guide the grader how deep it should go in the ditches, and they would drag it along.

So this was in the early '20s then that you are talking about.

Thelma Roehr, 69, Posey County

There was an old stagecoach road went from Evansville to New Harmony, and it went through here. Then this road was in bad shape and the wife of one of the commissioners belonged to my Wabash Homemakers Club and Raymond [husband] had to meet [my club members] down on the road and come across the field in a wagon so they could all come up here to club meeting. She went home and told him [her husband] it was time for me to have a gravel road, so he came out with a bunch of WPA's and they widened the road.

Vernell Saltzman, 81, Posey County

In the early part of 1900, Austin's father read in the paper where if the townships built the road, the county kept them up, so he called a meeting here at his home, in that room right over there. I guess it was full of men, and they decided to have an election to get gravel roads. So they had an election, and they voted gravel roads in.

And they said to him, "Now, Uncle Andy, you can have the first gravel road." Well, they decided it was senseless to build a road in the middle of the township, when it wouldn't hook on to any other road. So they built a road through Epsom and onto Elmore township line.

"Now, Uncle Andy, you can have the next road," but we had a commissioner from this township, so the next road was built there [by his house]. So Grandpa never got any road.

He died with a heart attack in 1911 and he never got a gravel road. The road was built in 1923, and I judge that was twenty years after Grandpa called that meeting.

Pearl McCall, 89, Daviess County

A team of mules rescue an early auto from deeply rutted roads.
Submitted by Whitley County

I remember quite well when my husband worked on what was known as State Road 29. Farmers didn't make much money and we needed extra money. He put a team of horses behind a dump scoop. He got $5 per day for him and the team of horses. Some days he worked with a pick and shovel for $3 a day. Then he and John Krienhop would spread straw over the newly-poured concrete with a pitchfork when the straw was brought in at night to keep the concrete from drying too fast. They got 25¢ per hour for this.

Everyone that lived along State Road 29 got flies and attic flies from this straw that was hauled in, so we had something to remember the laying of 29 for a long time. We are still fighting attic flies.

State Road 29 was changed to 421 several years ago.

Ethel Meyer, 78, Ripley County

It's not dusty like it used to be when we used to have gravel roads. The old gravel and dust would just get in your house and you could write your name anyplace.

Ellen McAfee, 68, Marshall County

Is there anything you would like to say, comparing your life [to years gone by]?

Yes, one big thing is tarvied [blacktopped] roads. Used to, you couldn't get your breath in the summertime. You had to keep your house closed up, it was so dirty and dusty. Oh, I've enjoyed [hard-surfaced] roads a lot.

Thelma Fox, 74, Shelby County

ON LAND, WITH FUEL POWER

Three women pushing a car through
almost impassable roads, while
the man steers.
Submitted by Marshall County

GASOLINE POWER

When they got the car[s], did they sell the horses, or did they keep them?

They [still] had the work horses, but they didn't have a buggy horse.

Thelma Nixon, 68, Union County

Hen Hardy was the first one to have an automobile. And, oh, we thought that was the most beautiful thing you ever saw. It didn't have no top on it and it was a big red car and the wheels was so big, and he'd come down the road with it and the dust would just be a-flyin'. Every time he would go past any of our houses, he'd squeeze that great big old ball of a horn and it would just toot so loud that the dogs and chickens would just go a-flyin'. They was just scared to death of it. He would think that was the smartest thing, because he could drive that along the road and people would come along with their horse and buggy, and the men had to get out and hold their horses 'til that automobile got by. The horses would jump around and almost break the shafts, they'd be so scared. They'd never saw anything like that.

What year would this be?

Oh, land, that must have been about 1905 or 1906.

Masa Scheerer, 82, Huntington County

Well, the first automobile ever I saw, I was in Churubusco. There's some men came from Ft. Wayne had been out to Blue Lake, and they went back through 'Busco and we was there and we happened to see them. Everybody was out on the street. Oh, (laugh), I just wish I had a picture of that automobile (chuckle).

Maggie Owen, 95, Whitley County

The first automobile came to town where I lived, we always said he got it off the dime store counter in Chicago, because it was such a rackety-looking thing. And it kept him busy, giving everybody in town a ride.

Hope Kessler, 86, Allen County

My uncle had a big buggy wheel affair that he called an automobile. It had an engine in it, and he would come over to the house. That was about 1910. We always enjoyed Uncle Dan's buggy automobile.

A Doctor Hess, the veterinarian, came to doctor the cows. That was the first automobile I had rode in. It didn't have a top in it, and just one seat. You know, he took me up the road for a whole mile and let me out to walk home. That was the longest mile I ever walked in my life, because we went so fast, and then I came home so slow.

Clara Nichols, 79, Wabash County

Can you remember the first automobile you saw?

Yes, it was a Ford, and our neighbors had it when I was about eight years old. I didn't get to ride in it, but the little girl whose Daddy had the car invited me over to set in the car with her one day, and I thought I was really doing something to set in that car.

Blanche Heaton, 82, Greene County

A lovely day for a drive on the back roads of Indiana. Note the two spare tires.
Submitted from Indianapolis District

I well remember the first automobiles that came into town. And then there was the first motorcycle. One of the fellows loafing in front of the store [saw the motorcycle] and said, "Well, those things [automobiles] are havin' pups."

Neva Schlatter, 79, Pulaski County

I remember when I was about four years old, my daddy and I took a walk over the farm. Our farm was one-half mile long, and we were almost to the upper end of the farm [when] my mother hollered and I heard her. We looked up and saw a dust storm, it was about a mile from where we were.

We could see it was an automobile coming, and I started to run; and believe it or not, I was back in time to see the automobile [go by]. We didn't see too many at that time, so this was quite a thrill.

My first automobile ride was with Dr. Whitlatch. He came to pick my mother up to take her down to my grandmother's, who had pneumonia. I got to ride along; and I was so thrilled, I didn't want to get out.

Pearl Snider, 76, Ripley County

The first automobile ride I ever had was when Mr. Welch and Mr. Griffith of the telephone company at Seymour brought their dogs and came down to our house to hunt quail. They would always take me and my cousin a ride up to Deputy.

We were afraid one time that we wouldn't get the dishes done in time, because they were going home, so we took mother's good coffee cups and saucers and we put them up in the top of the safe and didn't wash them until we came home. We were afraid if we didn't have our dishes done, they wouldn't let us go.

Juanita Hunter, 81, Scott County

My father bought his first new Ford car in 1914. Mort Enyart was bringing the car out from Fulton and my brother and I ran down the road, 'cause you could hear an automobile a mile away. And he stopped—it was a touring car—and before he could get the door open, why we had scrambled over the door and was sitting on the seat scared to death.

Lois Wagoner, 76, Fulton County

My Grandfather Hicks bought a new car and we were so thrilled with it. They came out one night and wanted to take us for a ride. We went to see my aunt and they had gone to an ice cream social.

I should explain something about the car first, or the story won't make sense. Cars, then, weren't like they are now, and the headlights wouldn't burn if the motor wasn't running. The men were all dressed in their overalls, and maybe not too clean, as far as that's concerned.

We went to this ice cream carnival where my aunt and uncle were. When we got ready to leave, Dad got out to crank the car—there were no self-starters then. He got out to crank the car, and when the motor started the lights came on; and he was embarrassed because it showed him in his overalls.

Thelma Robeson, 71, Fayette County

It was 1915 when he [father] got his car. It was a Crowell car. Boy, it was pretty. My brother, he'd take us all places. We'd go over to the Bluffton street fair and take the whole gang of the neighbor girls. The whole bunch of us would pile in. There'd be eight or ten of us kids would pile in that car. It was a big car, two seats, and we thought that was really something.

Masa Scheerer, 82, Huntington County

One day we saw a car coming from the north down past our house. There was a man in a buggy that had a team of mules hitched to it, and this car met the buggy. The car had that clanky horn on it, and it did make a lot of noise. The man with the buggy had to get out and hold his mules, it scared them so.

One other time this same fellow was down the road, and one of the mules laid down right out there in front of our car. They had quite a time until they had it up.

Alma Knecht, 78, Wabash County

We had a Chevrolet automobile. Our roads would get so bad in the winter, and it was made lower to the ground than a Ford was. So in the fall we'd put the car in the garage and left it all winter, till the roads got better, because it would drag until you couldn't get through the mud.

Then in the winter we went in a surrey wherever we went.

That was cold, but probably [either one] was cold?

Yes. I can remember well when we had the side curtains which was pretty floppy.

Catherine Summers, 67, Harrison County

We courted in an automobile, the kind that was open. It had flaps that came down in cold weather. You'd have to just really bundle up.

They didn't have a heater in them?

Oh, no, at that time they had a little charcoal heater that people used and they would also use heated bricks.

Evelyn Buchanan, 78, Scott County

When I went with one boy, we went up to Beech Grove Church, which was on top of Finley Knobs. We drove the car, and we almost had to get out and push, because the knobs were so steep that we couldn't get up [with] all of us riding.

Emma Baker, 78, Scott County

I used to work at a grocery store where they had the one-pump gasoline, so I would pump gasoline, too. I can remember selling gasoline five gallons for $1.00, that would be 20¢ a gallon.

Ellen McAfee, 68, Marshall County

An auto speed sign photographed in Brookston, in 1915. Note the $10.00 fine, very high in those days.
J. C. Allen Collection

I can remember sometimes on Sunday afternoon we'd take a little ride, and I can remember one time we went through a little village, and there was a sign up, "Speed Limit, Eight Miles an Hour." That was really something.

Grace Heinzman, 86, Hamilton County

There was a man from Waterloo Township, he had one of the first automobiles around. We thought he drove at terrible speeds. My grandmother said, "That man is going to kill himself driving so fast." The first car we had was an old Model T Ford and we sometimes wondered when we were going twenty-five miles per hour, if we weren't going too fast in that.

When I think of the Memorial Day [Indianapolis 500] races this year, I believe the qualifiers hit over two hundred as they were qualifying.

Harriet Gwinnup, 73, Fayette County

You know when you're driving a horse, they get tired, and you take pity on them. An automobile didn't get tired, but it did have flat tires. I don't think we ever ran out of gas but we did get flat tires.

Grace Heinzman, 86, Hamilton County

He [boy friend] had an old open Ford. He lived on a higher piece of ground about a fourth of a mile from here, and even in the winter when it was cold and with the doors closed, I could hear him start that Ford and I knew it was time for me to get my coat on and be ready to go.

It had the fenders rusted off—I mean at the top where the dirt had flew up on the fenders, it had rusted—and he had round pan lids wired over the holes in the fenders so that the mud wouldn't fly up on us. He was an inventor.

On the Fourth of July after he bought that Ford, two couples of us, after much talk and begging, got permission to drive to Edinburg on Sunday afternoon to see the Fourth of July performance.

We got less than two miles from home and we had a flat tire; we got another quarter of a mile and had a flat tire; and we had thirteen flat tires. Each time he had to take the tire off, patch the tube, put it back in the tire and put the tire on and pump it up. We didn't get to Edinburg, but we got home in time for church that night, or we wouldn't have gone again.

He carried his supplies for repair work right with him?

Everybody did. Well, some people could afford a spare tire, but he didn't have one.

Beulah Mardis, 76, Johnson County

I remember one time you were talking about race day in Indianapolis.

Oh, my, that was a great time, as a child! I suppose I was maybe six years old. We didn't have an automobile, of course. Automobiles were just coming into use and so many people from up north came to the races in their automobiles. So when that day came, when they would be going down—we called it the Michigan Road—it is 421 now. We lived about two miles west and Dad would hitch the horse and buggy and we would ride over to [the Michigan Road] and we would sit there in the buggy watching the cars go to the races. 'Course they had beautiful ones, we thought, and the women with their veils on. That was quite a sight.

Then we were a little more fortunate. In a year or two we moved over on the Zionsville Road, and they had a detour on 421, and all of those cars came down by our house. We took our chairs out in the front yard—tried to get all our work done up so we could do that—go out in the front yard and watch those cars go to the races.

And dust! Oh, it was just dirt roads and the dust was terrible, but we were so delighted to see those cars. I got more kick out of it than watching a parade today! That was really something!

Thelma Dye, 83, Boone County

Then I remember my husband bought our first car. It was a little Ford coupe runabout, with a running board. We had a hound dog that was part of the family, and the hound dog rode the running board, and that is the way we went. Old Queen was right there with us all the time.

Thelma Reedy, 80, Jay County

We got married in 1936, and the spring of '37 we bought a new Chevy, a four-door touring car, and I think we paid around $500 for it. We didn't have the money, but you went to the car dealer those days and they would make a note with you, and you would pay so much every month on this note there with them. They would hold it. We paid for that car before the note was due and we got it. I don't know how we did, but we did it.

Thelma Roehr, 69, Posey County

He bought a 1927 roadster, Model T. He had that before we were married, and he swapped it off and got that touring car that we had. And then we went on to one of those Model A Ford coupes with a rumble seat.

Do you want to tell me about the rumble seat?

Well, it was open, of course. The coupe part, you had the people set in front, but if you took anybody extra with you, they set back there in that little rumble seat. There wasn't any top on it, and they'd talk over that [wind]. So you didn't have anybody go with you on a real bad day or a cold day or anything.

Laura Drake, 72, Parke County

There was usually just one car per family, and if you went out with a boy, you were pretty sure you were going out in his father's car.

Gladys Tribolet, 70, Huntington County

It was during the end of the '30s when I started dating, and I remember I went to a Christmas Eve dance the DeMolays had with a boy, and his grandpa took us and came and got us and took us home. This boy didn't have a car and his grandpa wouldn't let him drive his.

Well-bundled against the dust and dirt, a
pretty woman drives a very early car.
Submitted by Rush County

Then when I started going with my husband who lived on a farm, he was making $10 a month working for the neighbors, so he bought a new car which at that time was $475 for a new Ford. The windshield rolled out on it and in the summer you rolled out the windshield to get all the air you could.

We went to the movies. You could go to the movies and buy a hamburger for one dollar. Gasoline, I know, was six gallons for one dollar, and whenever he had a little money saved, we might go to Indianapolis to the old Lyric Theatre to see a stage show.

Betty Alvey, 60, Howard County

We went together a year before we were married. That was in 1930 and 1931, the depression. I had a job doing housework. He didn't work steady, as jobs were almost impossible to find.

Finally he got a job selling gas and oil and heating oil from a tank truck. But he had to sell his car for a down payment on the truck. That was the hardest decision to make. No more rides in the car. Always the big ugly truck.

Mabel Hunter, 70, Jasper County

I was 15½ when I bought it. I was into driver's training when I saw this cheap car. It was a dark green and had one fender ripped back. The second "D" fell off in Dodge, so I rearranged the letters and made "dog" out of it.

The day I turned 16, that car was polished and ready, busted fender and all. I drove everybody all over town. I had this unfortunate habit of jumping curbs. You know, when you turn right, you always hop over the curb. That was great!

It was a neat car. I was going with a guy who bought me a fender that year for my birthday. He bought this fender and put a great big huge bow on it, brought it home and bolted it on for me. About a week later I was out with my girl friend in the car, and I wasn't used to that fender being there, and I turned around in the parking lot and came out, caught it, and ripped it back the same way that the old one was.

That was the greatest old car. I was really proud that I had done it myself.

What happened to it?

It finally just bit the dust. You know, it's only so long that an old car like that will last. It finally died—just collapsed.

Oh, the neat thing about that old car was the drag racing. You'd go downtown and sit next to a traffic light and everybody would go "brum, brum, brum" and when the light would change, you'd peel out.

It had a hole in the muffler, so it sounded like it had a great big engine. I'd have all these girls in the car, because nobody else had a car but me. Gas was a quarter a gallon then, so everybody would chip in a nickel or a dime, and we'd buy fifty cents worth of gas and that would take us for an evening.

We'd drive up and down Main Street, LaPorte, Indiana, and when we'd come to a light, it would sound like we would have this big powerful motor under the hood.

The guys would pull up next to me, and they'd say, "Hey, baby," then the light would change and they would go zoom, and I would go

putt, putt. They would be about three blocks away, and I'd be halfway
down the first block. That was fun.

Karren Saboski, 35, LaPorte County

LEARNING TO DRIVE

How did your life differ from your mother's?
Oh, I'm sure I did a lot of things that my mother couldn't do. For
instance, she never drove a car, and after we had been married, perhaps five or six years, we got a car. Then I drove the car and I would
go over and see her. As long as I knew my mother, she never drove a
car.

Della Ackerman, 77, Noble County

We had probably the fourth automobile in Jasper County. My husband went to Elkhart to buy it. The man came home with us and
taught us to drive. I became the first woman driver in the county.

Opal Amsler, 85, Jasper County

My uncle went to Indianapolis and drove a car back for one of the
neighbors and he [car dealer] told him how to start it and go home
with it, but he didn't tell him how to stop it. So when he got home he
couldn't stop, so he went around the block, and around and around
and around, until he ran out of gas, and then he stopped.

Hope Kessler, 86, Allen County

My husband was always particular about his tools. Everything had
to be in shelter, regardless of what kind of weather it was. He always
kept them so he had to push the storm buggy out to get the Ford out.
Now Oral [son] he was pretty quick to catch on [about the car], but
his dad wouldn't let him drive it, 'cause he wasn't old enough. So Oral
pushed the storm buggy out, [while father got the car out].
There's a wire fence in front, and so he kept backing out and he got
the Ford a-straddle of the shed and pushed the buggy a-straddle of the
fence, and he kept a-hollerin', "Whoa, whoa," to the Ford.
And Oral, he runs up and shuts off the motor and pulls the lever to
stop it. He stopped it, or it would still be a-going, I suppose, and I
razzed my husband after that, and I said, "He knew more about it than
you did." So we had a lot of fun.

Clara Carter, 100, Tipton County

The first car he got, my dad, he brought it home. He got it in the barnyard and he was going to drive it around, and he started toward the woodpile. "Whoa, whoa!!" but he just kept a-goin'.

Like he was driving horses?

And my dad never did drive. My mother did all the driving.

Bertha Pampel, 83, Benton County

A flat tire often required the unfortunate driver to remove the flat from the car and repair it by roughening the inner tube, applying an adhesive and a rubber patch. Then, after the patch had dried, the tube was pumped up by a hand pump and the tire was returned to the car.
Submitted by Switzerland County

My dad, some way, was never able to drive a car very successful, and we would get used cars, and he would have an accident.

So we didn't really have a car at our house until my sister was old enough to drive. We had old cars, and Dad had trouble with them, and he just gave up the driving to my older sister.

Alice Guyer, 68, Wabash County

Did your father have a car?

Oh, yes, but we weren't allowed to touch it. Nobody touched that but him.

Laura Drake, 72, Parke County

We started driving just whenever we was old enough to . . .

See over the steering wheel?

Yes, that's right.

Catherine Summers, 67, Harrison County

We didn't have any training, only what you would pick up from your parents or somebody.

You would go out in a field, as a usual thing, and drive around the wheat shocks to learn to drive and to miss them. That's the way you learned to drive your car.

Elsie Bossert, 70, Franklin County

Well, my father took me out one Sunday afternoon; explained all about the clutch and the brakes and shifting—hand shifting, of course—and after he had explained it all and showed me, probably three or four times, he told me to drive, and I drove around a four-mile square.

The next day I took my mother to a funeral, alone, so it didn't seem too hard. Well, one thing, the cars weren't complicated then.

And they didn't go as fast.

No, definitely not.

Virgie Bowers, 81, Pulaski County

We got our first automobile when I was twelve years old. And I learned to drive by backing it out of the driveway of the barn—we kept it in the barn—we didn't have a regular garage.

And I'd back it out and pull it up to the cistern and wash it and clean it. And one day I took a notion that if I could do that, I could drive it anywhere. So I drove down to my grandmother's, and Mother and Dad was so scared. They was standin' on the bank waitin' for me when I come back.

Ozetta Sullivan, 72, Harrison County

And then my brother when he was eighteen years old, my dad got him a car. And my sister, she said, "Well, I'm going to drive it, too." She says, "You took my cow and sold it and you bought my brother that car, and I'm going to drive it, too."

My sister, she said to me, "Let's get that car out of the garage and see where we can go with it." So we started out and we got down as far as the crossroads, just about a half mile, and I went to turn the thing around and we got it in the ditch. So, we had to push it out. We just worked like the dickens to get that pushed out, then I drove it back to the barn—back to our home.

But I never tried to put it in the garage. I suppose I would have went right through it. But that was the first car I ever tried to drive.

What year was this?

Well, I was about ten years old at that time, around 1910.

Masa Scheerer, 82, Huntington County

My niece always says, "Aunt Helen was born driving." My brother taught me to drive a Model T. I think I was only 12 years old, and he was very patient with me.

When I was in high school, I would drive and it [car] had to be cranked. Well, when I was starting home, the boys would always be over in the gym practicing basketball, and I had a friend (it wasn't the one who became my husband) and I don't know how he knew when I'd come out the door, but he'd always come over and cranked my car for me. Was I thankful!

Helen Weigle, 77, Tippecanoe County

My dad bought a car when I was 13 years old, and I learned to drive that car. And my brother, he taught me a lot about cars and how to drive, and so I learned all I knew when I was very young.

Did you have to get a driver's license?

No, no driver's license.

Bessie Werner, 80, Pulaski County

I'd drive the old horse and buggy, but I never wanted to drive a car.

So you never learned to drive?

No. One time my son and I were coming to town, and I had a basket of eggs and milk. He said, "Now, Mom, when I turn this wheel, you put your foot on that brake."

Well, I couldn't, and I just screamed. He grabbed the wheel and turned it back in. He said, "Now, Mom, don't never try to drive a car.

If you couldn't just put your foot on that brake, don't you ever [try to] learn to drive." And I never did want to.

Grace Hawkins, 93, Martin County

We had a car from the time we were married. I was learning. We kept the car across in the big barn, and I would drive it from the barn to the house. That was before you had to have a driver's license.

Richard said to his dad one day, "Eunice can get to driving and I won't have to go to town at all. I can just send her." He thought it would be so nice.

But Pap said, "You better keep her out of there," and I never touched that thing again. If I had had a wreck, I would have never heard the last of it.

Eunice Houze, 75, Ohio County

Road conditions at that time were mostly mud—some gravel. We had about 20 rods that wasn't even graveled to where our driveway was. So that's the way I learned to drive a car.

I would get in the seat behind the driver's wheel and Dorwin would—whether we were going to church, or anything—he would put on his rubber boots. He would get behind and push, and I would steer the car or guide it into the rut. All I had to do was to keep the car in the rut while he pushed until we got to the gravel part. That's where I learned to drive a car, in 1916.

Mary Yerks, 83, Allen County

I had never driven until I had a lot of cabbage, and I wanted my mother to help me make sauerkraut. It was the first time I had ever drove, but I had watched Albert drive. So I started out with my oldest son who was about one year old at the time, and I drove from Buck Creek to Otterbein. I drove through Battleground so I wouldn't have to be out on any big highways.

And I herded that old Model T and I got there. Sometimes I had to stop and think what I was supposed to do. My dad cranked it for me when I started to come back home, but I stayed two days, and we made sauerkraut.

Pearl Sollars, 70, Tippecanoe County

They [extension agents] came back from Purdue to teach us how to coldpack and prepare food and save it.

I drove a horse and buggy halfway, and I met up with Carlena Cowan Ramsey. She had a car. I could drive a car straight forward, but I could not back one. So I picked her up and Lena Thompson

Holler up, and Lena had one of those new-fangled coldpackers, and I drove the car to Farmersville School, and we worked all day canning.

When we got ready to go home, Carlena couldn't drive that car straight, but she could back it, so she backs it up, and we loaded Lena in with her precious coldpacker, and I drove the car home, and got my horse and buggy and come on home.

Is this why they are called cooperatives?

Oh, heck, I have laughed about that a many a time.

Vernell Saltzman, 81, Posey County

You know, now, you wouldn't think hardly of a lady not driving a car.

Oh, there are some your age that don't but, my, they're handicapped.

And there are some younger ladies who don't, and it just astonishes me when I meet them.

Virgie Bowers, 81, Pulaski County

TRAINS

I would stay two or three nights with Grandma Moore. They lived in this little town and one thing I do remember was hearing the trains at night, because we didn't hear that out on the farm. We didn't live close to the railroad.

But there in this little town, the trains would go through at night, and I remember hearing [them]. That would be the old steam engines that would make a lot of noise [with the] steam whistles.

Anna Martin, 79, White County

We had more fun when we'd go over the railroad track. We'd see a train a-coming and a lot of times we'd lay pennies, nails, or a shoe hook or something like that, and we'd let the train run over it. It would just mash it flat, and then we thought we had something.

My sister said, "Put Mom's scissors down, and see how they come out." So I put my mother's good scissors on the railroad track, that I had taken to school to cut out some things. You know, the train run over them and just mashed them flat, and if they didn't look awful.

When I took them home to Mom, she said, "You know, if you didn't know better, I'd feel sorry for you, because I'm going to paddle your butt and I'll paddle it good."

And I got a good lickin', enough I knew better. I should never have put her nice scissors on that railroad track and let the train run over them. But kids will do a lots of funny things.

Masa Scheerer, 82, Huntington County

When my husband was working in Hemlock, one attraction was the two trains that went through the town—one at four o'clock and one at seven o'clock. My girl friends and I would go meet the trains and see who would get on and off.

There wasn't much recreation at all at that time.

Edna Vandenbark, 92, Howard County

Large coal-fired steam locomotive on
the Monon Line which ran between
Chicago and Louisville.
Monon Collection
Indiana Historical Society Collection

Have you rode the trains a lot?

We used to ride that old C.B.&C. (chuckles). [We'd] go to Bluffton, from Huntington to Bluffton. We only had not quite a mile to walk to get to the Lee crossing, and then we'd flag it [train] down, and it'd stop and pick us up.

Mary Wolf, 88, Huntington County

How did you get to the state fair?

We went from Liberty on a train. We put our horses in the livery stable and got on the train and went to Indianapolis, stayed all day and came back at dark.

Delpha Borradaile, 91, Union County

You could get a train at Shoals and just take short trips? Like you could go to Washington for shopping and back the same day?

Oh, yes. When I was a child, I came to Loogootee [on the train] to take piano lessons. And we used to go on the train to Washington to the dentist, but we had to stay all night, because there wasn't any train after we got through at the dentist's office. We would get back in Shoals about 7 o'clock the next morning. We stayed at the hotel, the Meridian Hotel, and then I would get back in time to go to school.

Ruth Dye, 75, Martin County

When your father had his general store, did most of his supplies come by train?

Yes, most of them. There was what they called a local. That was a train that stopped at all the stations along the railroad. You ordered what you wanted from the different wholesale houses in Fort Wayne, and they shipped it out on that local. It stopped every morning at 8:30 or so. It left off the things that had been sent you, and you had to go to the depot and get them, and take them to the store and put them on the shelves.

That would have been before the telephone, too, wouldn't it?

Yes, mostly.

So most of his ordering was done by mail? That would be a long process.

Yes, it took two or three days. 'Course, there was some things, like bread, that you automatically got on certain days, like maybe Monday and Wednesday.

Agnes Emenhiser, 90, Allen County

[Mrs. Bell was postmistress in a small post office for many years.]

One mail carrier came in one evening about four o'clock and left the mail and started home.

And, oh, I heard the train whistling down the track, just a ways west of here, and it just whistled and whistled and whistled and whistled. And I wondered, and about that time there was a trainman came running and came into the Post Office and said, "Your mail carrier just got hit by the train and his little boy was with him."

And he said, "The train is going on and is going to meet at Lincoln

City with another train there, and they are going to take him [little boy] to Evansville." And that was little Russell Masterson.

And he said, "You'll have to go over," because he had carried the mail. I'll never forget it, I'll tell you. Waldo, the carrier, was hit [and dead], and they left him laying on the floor over there. Well, in those days they didn't have ambulances, they didn't have doctors. And he was cut, blood all over the floor . . . oh, I'll just never forget it.

Did they recover?

Oh, no, Waldo was killed. The train killed him and the one horse, but the little boy recovered. The little boy's still living.

There was, oh, ever so long after that, when that train would whistle that I would just jump. That was a tragedy.

Eldo Bell, 86, Spencer County

Then, when the boys got old enough to work away from home, they went north to pick corn a couple of falls, and after that they stayed all the time.

Then they wrote back to the folks and told them about quite a bit of building being done in the northern part of the state, and, as my father was a carpenter, we decided that we'd move to the north part of the state.

Then the freight car took our cow and our chickens up. Mom always kept 150 Leghorn hens, and our cow and our chickens and our furniture went north.

My brother that was two years older than I was decided to go with them, because somebody had to go in the car to feed the chickens and take care of the cow, and everything, and he decided to go.

We had to stop at Reynolds and wait five hours there for a train to go on to Remington—that's where we were moving to. When the train got to Reynolds, there was a Y switch where they had to switch the freight cars off to meet another train at 5:00, and they thought the switch was empty. But it had his car already there, and they give my brother's car a big boost, and it got to the end of the Y, and it killed him. Skinned our cow quite a bit, broke our sewing machine, broke our chair and killed him instantly. And that's the way we arrived at Remington.

Grace Elrod, 85, Jasper County

We had more fun when we was going to school. If it would be bad weather, my mom she would hitch up the horse and come over and get my brother, sister and I, and we brought our two cousins along home.

We were all in the buggy, and it was muddy as all get out, and when we went by, some of the kids throwed stones at the horse and hit it.

And away we went, just a-sailin', and we had to go over the railroad track and a train was coming. My mom tried to slow the horse down, to let the train go by.

But that horse, she couldn't hold him, and she'd keep a-saying, "Whoa, Jimmy!! Whoa, Jimmy!!" and us kids was all hollering and laughing. We just went over the railroad track a-bouncin', and the train went by.

And Mom says, "I'll never come after you any more." She says, "Just walk home, it's only 2½ mile." So after that, we always walked home.

Masa Scheerer, 82, Huntington County

Travel by train at that time was the main way of travel for most people. I usually took a sleeper, you know, a sleeping car. On these sleeping cars, [when] your bunk isn't made up, the seats in the day are just like any car.

[They] had compartments, too. These little compartments were really nice. It had a little door that you lifted up and you put your shoes in it, that you wanted polished. It even had a toilet. And the sleeping berth was very comfortable.

Anna Martin, 79, White County

August 11, 1966, my sister, Grace Cheever, Mabel Hunter and myself went to the National Home Economics Conference in Colorado. We left from the Union Station in Chicago on the Burlington Zephyr. Grace and I sat in the dome car the whole time—we never left. We enjoyed the scenery and it was just great. When we arrived in Colorado Springs, we hadn't slept enough, so we went to bed at six o'clock that night.

Florence De Young, 68, Jasper County

Do the trains still go through?

Yes, the trains still go through, but there are very few passenger trains still left on the—Amtrak, now, I guess they call it.

And that has made a lot of difference in small towns, too. There used to be a lot of train transportation.

Agnes Emenhiser, 90, Allen County

INTERURBANS AND TROLLEYS

I do miss the interurban. We used to have that.

Evelyn Buchanan, 78, Scott County

Our community was really progressing when an interurban line was built between Kendallville and Ft. Wayne. Men moved in with horse-drawn machinery to do the grading for the tracks. The powerhouse was located in Kendallville in Sunnyside. Power was generated there to run the trolley. The turntable was located just east of South Main Street. That was the end of the line, so we would have to walk on uptown, or take a taxi.

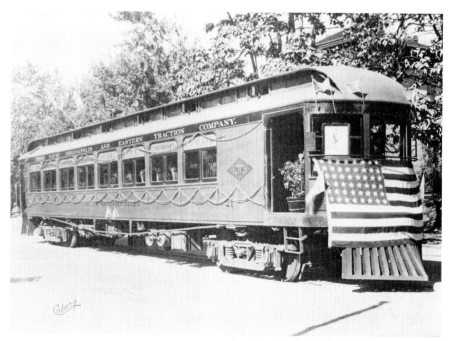

A trolley car belonging to the Indianapolis and Eastern Traction Company. It is decorated in honor of James Whitcomb Riley's birthday, with the poet's picture in the front window.
Indiana State Library

The fare was 5¢ from Fairbanks Corner to Avilla, 10¢ to Kendallville and 55¢ to Ft. Wayne.

When the first passenger car was run, it was a great sight, and many people came to see this wonderful car which could take them to the city of Ft. Wayne in an hour and a quarter.

Lucile Imes, 82, Noble County

I went to Mt. Vernon High School, and we had a trolley car that went by where the railroad track is.

You mean it went down the railroad track?

It was right beside, north, of the railroad track; but not very far, maybe twenty-five feet or so.

Now is that the same thing as a traction line? I've heard that expression.

Right. The trolley has to have a [power] line on top. Anyhow, we had to walk down there early in the morning. Sometimes it was mighty cold to walk from home down there.

A mile and a half?

At least a mile. We used to wear galoshes. There was a store down there, and I used to leave my galoshes there. We would get on the traction and then they would stop—like at Ford Station, and there was a store in Caborn where people could wait and get on the traction—I forget all the names of the crossings.

Then we went on in to Mt. Vernon, and the car barn was down on 4th and Main.

Did it turn around at that point?

Well, it backed up at Walnut and turned around there. There was a real car barn where they would take these cars in and clean them up and do work on them—whatever they had to do to maintain them.

Thelma Roehr, 69, Posey County

My Grandmother Armstrong lived in Marion. The streetcar ran at her house and turned at her corner. Many customers on the streetcar would stop at her corner and visit with her. We used to take common pins and nails and put them on the track to see them flattened.

Betty Trout, 62, Blackford County

I remember one time when Madeleine was a baby, we put her in the go-cart [baby carriage] and walked two and a half miles to the inter-urban line to catch a car to go to Kokomo to a baseball game.

Edna Vandenbark, 92, Vanderburgh County

When there was an away-from-home basketball game at Tipton, we'd ride the interurban to Tipton, about twenty miles. I think it cost 15¢ to ride that interurban.

I had an aunt and cousin that lived in Tipton, so we were well-acquainted with the interurban. We'd go down there on Friday, and stay 'til Sunday, and then come back. When you rode the interurban, it swayed—back and forth, back and forth.

One time my sister and I had gone to Tipton for the weekend, and our parents were to come after us on Sunday. I think I could ride for half price, because I was under 12. They told us if they didn't call by noon on Sunday, or come by noon, we were to catch the interurban back to Kokomo—the first one that came after lunch on Sunday. Well, we waited and waited, and just at twelve o'clock they drove in, so we didn't have to catch the interurban to come back home.

Just as we were getting ready to come home, people called in from Sharpsville to say there had been a terrible accident on the interurban line. Two had collided, and several people were killed and burned. I guess it was just our luck not to ride it that day. Our fate certainly would have been changed.

We didn't have many automobiles during the depression. I think maybe one car would go down [our street] in a day or so. In the wintertime when there was deep snow, we could walk out on the [street] car tracks in the middle of the street, and maybe you could walk for blocks and blocks, and never meet an auto.

Betty Alvey, 60, Howard County

The interurban was out here when we moved out in the country in 1920. We made very good use of it, because while the mister was gone on his job, if I wanted to go to town, we just walked over to the interurban and went. Then our daughter went to high school, and she rode the interurban to high school.

Hope Kessler, 86, Allen County

We had a neighbor lady who liked to get out, and take the interurban to Kendallville, and get drunk. This happened about every three weeks. I remember a trip that was hazardous.

It got icy, and when she came home, she had difficulty getting up the hill. She had purchased a hamper of bananas. My dad knew she was having difficulty and came to her rescue. He brought her in the house, with her bananas, to wait until he could hitch up the horse to the buggy and take her home.

She tore the hamper open and started throwing bananas all around the room. I had more bananas to eat that day than I've ever had. I thought she was great.

Lucile Imes, 82, Noble County

What did you do before the streetcar? There wasn't any public transportation, was there?

We walked, and in the country they had a horse and buggy.

Do you remember when they quit using streetcars? What did they do then?

We went to buses. And they just stopped city buses a few years ago. I imagine eight or nine years since they stopped buses.

Hazel Dolkey, 78, Knox County

When I moved into Wabash, we had city streetcars and city buses. And they wanted to take the track up and take the [street] cars off, because they didn't pay. And we tried to tell them to keep it, but we had no foundation, 'cause it didn't pay.

Then the automobiles came along, so that stopped that.

Alvah Watson, 97, Allen County

The trolley car, the streetcar, as we knew it, came into existence and out of existence.

Isabel Schoeff, 81, Huntington County

That was a nice form of transportation. I'm sorry we don't have it anymore. It only lasted such a short time. It was nice.

Hope Kessler, 86, Allen County

IN THE AIR

Amelia Earhart on Purdue campus with
her plane and a number of girl students.
Purdue University

AIRPLANES

We came along with the horse and buggy, then, of course, the automobile. And now we're up in the air.

Alvah Watson, 97, Allen County

Did you have any heroes or heroines that you liked?

Lindbergh was at his height during my high school years, and I had boy cousins which were just thrilled with aviation and all the things they were doing with airplanes, so I suppose I remember Charles Lindbergh best.

Alice Guyer, 68, Wabash County

I remember when the first airplane come, when I was just little. It lit down there at Warren, and everybody went to see it. That was the greatest thing ever was, you know! (laughter) And the people all went down to see that airplane, I remember that.

Cora Keplinger, 80, Huntington County

They used to take people on trips from the airport in Connersville. You would go up and pay a penny a pound to fly. They would take you up.

My brothers always tried to get me to go, because they always wanted to know how much I weighed. I didn't want them to know about how much I weighed.

Harriet Gwinnup, 73, Fayette County

Have you ever been on a plane?

One time, out at the airport. It was on Mother's Day. Both my boys were in World War II, and they were both in airplanes. When my oldest son came home, out at the airport they were giving free rides to mothers for Mother's Day.

And Clarence [son] said, "Mom, I want to take you up in the airplane." And I said, "Oh, Clarence, I didn't think I'd ever want to go in a plane." He said, "Well, I'd like to take you." And I said, "Well, if you want to take me, I'll go."

So we went to the airport and when we got ready to go, I said, "Well, I say, if we don't come back, just send me some red roses."

So we came back, but that's the only time I was ever in an airplane. And I didn't go no more.

If you had a chance to take a space ride to the moon, would you go?

No, ma'am! It didn't take me long to say that!

Lulu Rheinhardt, 91, Vanderburgh County

Have you ever flown?

Yes, I enjoyed it. My sister and her husband wanted to take me along and I spent one month with them. I flew from New York to Ohio.

I was on a nice big plane, and they helped me into a seat where I could look out over the earth. It was beautiful. It was far different than what you can see from the ground. That large plane, that was like setting in your rocking chair in your living room. It was great.

Alma Knecht, 78, Wabash County

I have never flown, and I don't believe I ever will, the way I feel now. It would have to be an emergency, I'm sure of that.

I went on most every other kind of transportation: motorcycles, automobiles, horse and buggy, horses and sleigh, boats, buses, trains, a whole lot of things, but never in an airplane.

Hope Kessler, 86, Allen County

And now here in the 1980s, my husband became 53 years old and he decided to take up flying. So he got his flying lessons and became a pilot and bought his own airplane. And our leisure time now is flying.

I can't say that I'm that fond of it, but he likes it real well and if it means being together, why that's what it's all about. And then our daughter will go if she can take a friend with her, and it does hold four people, so that is our leisure time here at home.

Mary Ann Hoskins, 49, Grant County

What do you think about space travel?

It's all beyond me. Old as I am, I just can't understand what they're trying to do. 'Course, that is what we used to say about airplanes, and we had our own planes and flew.

You had your own planes, in your family?

My husband and I did, when we had Ash Petroleum Company uptown here. He had a terminal down at Madison, and so we took long jaunts.

Did you fly the plane?

No, just went for the ride.

Mary Ash, 84, Shelby County

My husband grew up in Brown County and walked to school, or sometimes rode a horse. He traveled very slowly and very little.

Since we have been married, he has commuted to Washington for a day's work, having breakfast with me and the evening meal with me.

That is simply an example of how things have moved so much faster now.

Dorothy Kelley, 64, Hendricks County

And we think nothing at all of getting on the airplane and in just a few hours you can be in Arizona or California, Florida or in England.

Helen Samuelson, 57, Marshall County

This is one way it seems like it is a small, small world, because you'll get somewhere far, far away, and maybe you'll find your next-door neighbor right there with you.

It is a small world when you find people so far away, yet so close.

Alma Small, 61, Dubois County

Large crowds came out to the airfields to
see the new airplanes.
Submitted by Newton County

It takes four hours and you can be from Chicago to San Francisco. But I think that if you travel by plane, you miss out on seeing a lot of the countryside, and meeting people from different parts of the country.

I've been to California, but I really haven't been in California, because we were just there in the airport, and it doesn't seem like you've been there.

Transportation is so much faster than it once was, and I guess that's the way it is with our whole life. We're just moving at a rate of speed about the same as an airplane.

Floy Jacobus, 53, Gibson County

SPACE TRAVEL

How about space travel, do you understand what this is about?
Oh, yes! I've read every bit of it, and watched it on TV, and I love it. I'd love to go.

You'd love to go on a spaceship?
Oh, yes, if I wasn't 72 years old, I might even take flying lessons.

But wouldn't it frighten you?
Oh, no!!

Opal Gallagher, 72, Shelby County

Thoughts on space travel?
Well, it's a wonderful invention, but I'm just wondering about it and if they'll really accomplish what they hope to. Of course, Columbus wasn't admired when he was working with ships.

I hope it will be better than we had thought it would be. And the ones who make those trips are certainly brave men.

Mary Gleason, 87, Perry County

Maybe we haven't seen the good that will come from that [space travel] yet. They talk about how it's really going to be a benefit to us. With the population growth now, we may not have the room on this planet for all these people. We may have to live out there. With the space shuttle, I think it is going to be easier to travel.

'Course, I'm not buying a ticket yet (chuckles).

Verlee Jochum, 64, Dubois County

What does the space age mean to you?
I was just amazed when that first one went up. I just sit there and watched and I just couldn't hardly believe it. It was something, and I did say some prayers (chuckles).

How has it affected you since?
I suppose I kind of got used to it, 'cause they been sending up so many. But it's a vast spread between the horse and buggy days and I've seen all that.

Cora Keplinger, 80, Huntington County

And now we are into the space age. Most amazing. I often think my grandparents would be so unbelieving of the space shots and this type of thing. Some believe we are tinkering with the wrong things—we are getting too far out into God's territory.

Verona Lemmon, 65, Daviess County

We have space travel today. I don't know what the outcome will be. I guess if it wasn't meant for us to explore outer space, we wouldn't have been given the intelligence to do it.

When Columbus discovered America, lots of people thought that was unnecessary and foolish, too. But if someone hadn't pursued it, we wouldn't know the world is round.

Nellie Frakes, 71, Perry County

I can get interested if I think there might be people out there that they could get in contact with. That kind of fascinates me, to think about how big the universe is, and that maybe there are other people out there.

Margaret Daubenspeck, 57, Rush County

I will never forget the day the men walked on the moon, because it just seemed like it was one of the most thrilling things that could happen.

Did you see them walking on the moon on television?

Oh, sure, yes!!!

Helen Sauser, 64, Wayne County

I have a lot of respect for those men who did that. They didn't know when they left the earth whether they would ever get back or not, and they were really brave to do it.

Mary Yerks, 83, Allen County

I think it is wonderful they can do it. But, on the other hand, to me it seems like a lot of money. I'd like to see 'em work more on cancer, spend more money on that.

It's wonderful that they went to the moon. I think it's wonderful, but don't seem to me that they have to keep a-going every other year.

Thelma Fox, 74, Shelby County

Did you ever think that while you still lived that somebody would walk on the moon?

I tell you, it is so far beyond what you can comprehend. Now our children aren't going to feel that way. It is a little like the new garage door opener. I am just amazed, but my three grandchildren sit and wait for the garage door to open. It never crosses their mind that you had to get out and open it.

So, what is miraculous to us is common everyday to them.

Joan Ford, 49, Jay County

As my husband says, he wonders what is going to happen in the next 25 years. We've seen a lot in 50 plus years, and he was wondering what our children were going to see in the next years.

We have a grandson, his desire is to be a spaceman. He is always in outer space. He is only ten years old, but he thinks of airplanes and spaceships all the time.

Alma Small, 61, Dubois County

What are the most significant changes in American society during your lifetime?

I think when you have gone from horse and buggy to outer space travel, you have covered a good many miles. A lot of wonderful things have happened and most things have changed since I was young, but that seems like the most outstanding thing.

Elizabeth McCullough, 68, Putnam County

I'll never forget how we used to go and kinda hide when we'd see one [auto] coming, because we were afraid one might hit us. They'd go so much faster than we did. They'd go ten miles an hour, and we only went one step at a time.

Now you travel so fast that you can go down to Fort Wayne and have lunch at 12 o'clock and have your dinner tonight at 6 o'clock in Miami, Florida.

So when you see a person going down the highway now, I often think what they used to say, "When you see him a-going you think he ought to be coming. He's behind time, he's going so fast."

Alvah Watson, 97, Allen County

BOMBS AND BAD TIMES

Homemakers Look at History

"It was hard, but we got through. You just did the best you could."

Elma Matthew

N ational and international events bring with them many changes in daily life, some short-lived and some long-term. This section looks at those changes through the eyes of homemakers.

World War I came to a country which had been at peace for many years. Homemakers watched as neighbors and relatives left in uniform for an unknown fate, while those left behind worked hard to support the war effort. Victory brought the soldiers home, but life had changed. Morals, values and lifestyles were never quite the same again.

In the twenties, women bobbed their hair and wore short skirts. Bootleg liquor and smoking were fashionable, and the Ku Klux Klan was an influential part of Hoosier life.

In the thirties, the Great Depression brought financial distress everywhere, and the homemaker's role was especially important as she conserved every family resource—cash, food or clothing.

The forties eased financial problems, but brought another war, World War II. Once again mothers and wives waited and worried at home as the young men of the community left for the armed services. Rationing and shortages were everywhere, and everyone worked to take the place of the departed young men in the offices, factories and farms.

In 1945, an uneasy peace settled over the world, broken by small wars in Korea and Viet Nam—smaller, but just as tragic for those involved.

Through all these world events, homemakers worked to keep their home and family life intact and to help their nation.

WORLD WAR I

World War I soldiers on a troop train.
Submitted by Tipton County

You see, we had never been in war and everybody was so moved by the war. You can't remember that, because you have had war all your life since that time. Everyone that has come along has been involved, afraid we are going to have war, or we do have a war, or something. But when the first World War came, that was such a new thing. See, we hadn't been involved since the Civil War—the Spanish-American, but very few went to that.

Our hearts were broken when the boys had to go. We would follow them in Mt. Vernon and see them get on the train. We would have bond meetings at all the schools in the country. And Roy and I always liked to sing, and we would sing patriotic songs. People would save their pennies and come in there to buy bonds. Everybody, everybody, I don't mean just a few in the neighborhood. Everybody came from miles around with their money to buy bonds.

Everybody cooperated. They would come and ask you what you would do—how many hours would you knit—and we would sign up to do so many hours of knitting and different things like that.

But then, prices also rose on the farm, and especially hogs. We made more money with hogs than anything, because the prices rose so at that time.

Did you lose a lot of your friends during the war?

Yes, quite a few. And every time another group would have to go, we were sure that he [husband] would have to go, and he wasn't called. Then one of the board members told us it was because of what he was doing in farming. That helped us understand, because he wanted to go. He would have gone. He would have been glad to go.

I guess you remember the day the war ended.

Oh, I should say. We came down to my dad's and we hunted up all of the sheep bells, cow bells, everything that we had, to tie on the car.

They were so patriotic in that day. That's why I say we lost so much in so many ways today.

Audrey Blackburn, 86, Posey County

Mother had an aunt and a cousin near Bunker Hill, and we would go visit them periodically in our Model T Ford. My brother and this cousin would play the piano, and they'd sing the war songs. I can remember them playing "Over There" and "Oh, Johnny, Oh!"

Beulah Grinstead, 68, Hamilton County

In World War I, I think they were more patriotic at that time than we are today. Everybody had a flag. You were very disappointed if you didn't have one.

My father stayed up almost all night to fix the automobile so it would start, to take our neighbor boy to Versailles for his examination.

Pearl Snider, 76, Ripley County

Being born in 1913, I was very young; but my uncle, Clifford Jenkins, joined the Army when he was sixteen. He was not married yet, and Mother's home was his home, because my grandmother [his mother] had died.

He would come to our house and talk about many far-away places which seemed to me to be so far away that I would never, never see them in my lifetime.

Beulah Grinstead, 68, Hamilton County

When World War I started, Roy [brother] and Ray [brother] had been staying at home and doing the farming for Dad 'cause he didn't have very good health.

Well, when the war came, Roy enlisted and Ray stayed home to do the farm work. He got exempt.

Then when Roy came home, after the war was over, Ray got married and went to farm by himself. And then Roy, he got married, and then he stayed home and helped farm with Dad.

Anna Martin, 79, White County

My husband was at Camp Taylor; he never got any further than Camp Taylor. My husband had done office work, and they made him work in the office. But the group that went from Floyd County, they were sent over. They were in France when the Germans let them have it, and a couple of them were injured.

Mary Flispart, 81, Floyd County

In the first World War, Guy was farming and I was gonna have a baby, and he couldn't get off. And we had to go to the judge and, well, I was so embarrassed. The judge said to me, "Are you going to have a baby?" Well, that embarrassed the life out of me. People didn't talk like that then. Well, I think he looked at me and said, "Expect so!" But Guy didn't have to go.

Bertha Pampel, 83, Benton County

My brother was in World War I. He was in France, and he was with the military police, so after the war was over, they kept him over there quite a while, helping get things straightened around again.

The war was over in November, and he came home in July, the second of July. And, oh, you never saw so much excitement around our house as when he came home. We were so thrilled.

Helen Weigle, 77, Tippecanoe County

My brother was one of the first volunteers in our county. He was 21; he would have been drafted and taken anyway. But he enlisted and served two years in the war, eleven months of which was spent in France. He was in the three big battles. I can't remember the names of all of them, but the Marne was one.

His recollections of the war were quite traumatic—sleeping with a gas mask on and sleeping in foxholes, trenches or dugouts, sometimes to wake up and find your buddy had died in the night from wounds. It was all very terrible.

When my brother returned from the service, he was handicapped because he contracted tuberculosis from his experience in the war. He died at the age of 34. Many young men from our area lost their lives or lost their health.

Mary Graver, 80, Wayne County

My husband was in the war, World War I, and he was gassed. He was 100% disabled.

When we first found out, the children were real little. Dwight was about eight and Janie about five years old. It was when we were on the big farm.

He went through the clinic at Cincinnati, and they found he had a hole in his lung, about the size of a teacup. We thought he had coughed all the time because he smoked cigarettes.

They told him not to work anymore. But he had a family, he had a crop out and couldn't get any help, and he had to work. They wanted him to take a pension, but he wouldn't. The crops brought in more than they would allow him for disability.

Mona Winkler, 84, Knox County

What do you remember about the first World War?

Well, I had three brothers in the first World War. One of them was turned down, because he had a crippled hip. The other two, one was in the Navy and one was in the Army.

But I had one brother that was in the war and he was shell-shocked. He had a pretty rough time of it when he got home. One time, in 1938, he left home one morning and he drove his car around in front of the house and set in the car for a little while, so a man told us, and then he went away.

We weren't able to find him. We went to Peru, where he was supposed to be going, and we found his sample case—he was a salesman—and we found a restaurant where he went in about 9:00 and told the folks, "I think I'll have a cup of coffee." And after they waited on him, he said, "I think I'll just eat my dinner while I'm here." So, they said, he ordered his dinner, but he didn't eat it. He got up and left.

He was gone for twelve days, and we couldn't find him. They found his car finally. He had had one of those spells, you know. That was one thing that was bad about the war.

We finally found him. He came to himself, and he was standing on the sidewalk in the rain, and he was looking in the window in one of the stores, and he said to a man, "What town is this?" and he said, "It's Oklahoma City." And he said, "When's Christmas?" The fellow said, "It was yesterday."

So he found a way to get to Tulsa, Oklahoma. My sister lived there and she got him and put him to bed. When she found him he was down to the hotel, and she told them to hold him there. She found he had a long beard; he had someone else's sweater; he had book matches from Alabama and different places he had been.

And he told me afterwards, "If you ever come see me, and you don't find me in the house, you look under the bed, 'cause I'll never leave this house." It scared him so. He lived a little while, but he died from a heart attack. It was all caused from the war.

Alvah Watson, 97, Allen County

WORKING ON THE HOME FRONT

World War I started when I was a senior in high school. It interrupted the educational process significantly, because so many men teachers were taken. I know I was not privileged to take typing, because our business teacher was taken into service.

Mary Graver, 80, Wayne County

World War I had started, and almost all our teachers were women.

Violet David, 82, Brown County

I graduated in 1915 and I was fortunate to get work at Natco, National Automatic Tool Company. It made two stenographers when I went there. They had a bookkeeper, and a man in charge of engineering. They were all men. William Bockhoff was the president, and the owner of it, and they had a vice president and a secretary, all men.

I made $5.00 a week when I started. I worked there five years during the war period. When I quit to get married (because married women weren't allowed to work in offices then) I was making $35.00 a week, which was excellent money.

They raised us fast during the war, because we worked until midnight. I learned the dictaphone. Natco was the first company to have the dictaphone installed, and I used that. When I would go back to work in the morning, my desk would be filled with rolls for the dicta- phone. They were round and about six inches tall. Then you would transcribe them on the typewriter, and when you got through, they would be ready for them to dictate on again.

We worked real hard, I was fortunate to get that. I worked there until I was married in 1919.

Donna Parker, 83, Wayne County

Two years after we were married, World War I came along. I had begun, little by little, taking over jobs outside and helping Austin do a lot of things.

That year of World War I, they [draft] took our hand [hired man]. We kept a hand the year around, but he was conscripted and had to go. We couldn't keep them out. He was the age to go, one of the first ones to go.

So I just made a hand on the farm, and Grandmother [husband's mother], she did the cooking.

Was Austin's father living at that time?

No, he died in 1913.

Pearl McCall, 89, Daviess County

Father was poorly in 1918. We had a hired hand [who was drafted] so that left us without any help. We girls—I was about 16 then—we got our corn in. We had it to roll and we had it to plow. We plowed with a mule team, and I guess we did a fairly good job, because an old bachelor neighbor came over and inspected the work, to see what kind of a job we were doing.

And I guess I done most of all kinds of work on the farm.

Hazel Williams, 79, Franklin County.

I went out to a one-room school and taught; had eight grades the first year. And the flu broke out in 1918, and I had signed up to teach that year again. The flu was so bad that the government put out a plea for nurses. I had always had a longing to be a nurse or a butcher (laughs), so I signed up to go as a nurse.

I signed up in July, and Washington sent me word, even called me on the telephone, and wanted to know how soon I would be ready to go. I said I would get ready as soon as I could get my clothes done.

I had to make my own uniforms. They sent directions for the uni- forms, and told me just what I was to do. No money—they furnished nothing for them. So you had to do it all yourself.

I told them it would take a week to get the things done. The neighbors came in and helped me make the clothes. I got ready, and then waited and waited and waited.

They said don't come until we send your transportation. The day after the Armistice was signed, the tickets came for me to leave. I was to go to Fort Oglethrope, Georgia, and I left the next day.

An early office worker. Note adding
machine in foreground.
Submitted by Whitley County,
L. M. Huffman, photographer

There were thirty in our class, and we were not very well received, because we were a young group of women from all walks of life. Teachers and a little bit of everything. Down there, they were all older nurses, and, of course, that was a doctors' camp completely, a medical camp. To have a young group come in like that—quite attractive ones—we made quite a stir. We were invited to parties they had for us, so we had a lot of fun along with the hard work.

I was there until the last of February. The young man I was engaged to got out of service on New Year's Day and come home. I had promised him I would ask for my discharge as soon as he got out. They had put that clause in when I signed up, that I would ask for my discharge when he got out. So they gave it to me.

I was longer getting out than I was getting in. I came home and we was married March 19, 1919. Then I went to the farm and have lived on the farm ever since.

Margaret Butler, 87, Steuben County

World War I was different. I was in high school at that time, and it was a time that we would always remember, because of all the boys being sent to the army. We'd go and meet the train. They'd dismiss us from school, and we could all go to the train and see them.

We had a lot of cousins and boyfriends, and we all got to visit the Army camp. Most of our boys from here went to Fort Knox, Kentucky. That was a big day for a group of girls to take boxes of fried chicken and cookies and pies and get on the interurban car and go to Fort Knox and stay all day on Sunday. All the Scott County boys would come and eat with us.

Zelma Blocher, 81, Scott County

I used to go to Camp Taylor with a group that sang. We would put on a little show at the camp.

Mary Flispart, 81, Floyd County

That was the time you made a quilt; you paid a dime for a block and you put your name on the quilt block. Then this went to the Red Cross.

Pearl Snider, 76, Ripley County

I joined the Palmyra Home Economics Club during the first World War.

All the women from the Palmyra Church, the Royal Oak Church and the Upper Indiana (which I went to) met at Frichton, up above Snider's grocery store, to sew pajamas for soldiers. The women in Frichton brought their machines, and we were there, and then we just waited and waited for the man and lady from Vincennes to bring the material, which was outing flannel.

Anyway, when we came back the next time, we decided to have the first Home Economics Club there in Frichton. They chose my aunt to be the first president.

Did you do other things for the soldiers?

Our church women met at our house and sewed with three machines.

They would spend the day at our house and sew. We pressed and folded those pajamas and turned them in. I don't know how many socks Momma knit. I didn't know how, so I got out of that.

Mona Winkler, 85, Knox County

Did the women do any sewing for servicemen?

Opal: My mother made shirts. She went to Jeffersonville and got them by the bundles and they had a place in Scottsburg where she took them and got her money. Then she'd pick up her next bunch.

I had a new machine, and I made bed sacks for the army, because I would whip them up in a little bit, and it didn't take as much work.

Mother liked to make shirts, and she just made bundle after bundle.

Juanita: I made helmets and sleeveless sweaters to go under their jackets in World War I. Khaki helmets.

Juanita Hunter, 81, and Opal Whitsett, 84, Scott County

FOOD

What effect did World War I have on your family and community in general?

Well, we had all kind of heatless days, sweetless days, wheatless days; and we couldn't get any white flour, so we made bread of all kinds of rice flour, potato flour, rolled oats, rye flour, bran, corn meal, and all kinds of grain.

Did the Extension Service teach lessons how to make that bread?

Yes, they did.

Hazel Thomas, 81, Parke County

I remember during the first World War we were exchanging recipes where we used different kinds of flour; corn flour, rice flour, and potato flour—all kinds of different flour and different kinds of ingredients from what we were used to in our baking.

I remember trying out the different kinds in baking cookies and different types of baking. Of course, sugar was rationed, too, so we really had to improvise in a lot of ways.

What was the purpose of changing to a different type of flour?

Well, that was on account of the wheat was being used for our soldiers in the baking of bread overseas.

In making a recipe, types of flour were much different, you see, in the way of thickening.

Iva Crouse, 85, White County

My mother baked all our bread. During the war years you couldn't get white flour, and I remember her making bread from rye flour. We were skeptical at first, but after we ate it a while, we got used to it.
 Lois Wagoner, 76, Fulton County

We used a lot of graham flour, it was called then.
 Mary Graver, 81, Wayne County

If you bought a 25-pound sack of flour, you had to take maybe ten pounds of corn meal, or they wouldn't let you have the flour at the grocery store. And I always had more corn meal than I needed. But that didn't hurt us any to use a little corn meal. I learnt to bake real nice corn bread, I tell you that.
 Mary Wolf, 88, Huntington County

During WWI we got potato flour and rice flour, and they were horrible stuff.
 Maud Sloneker, 90, Fayette County

And sugar was almost a nonentity.
 Mary Graver, 81, Wayne County

I remember baking cookies for a meeting, and when a lady saw these cookies, she said, "Who in the world had enough sugar to bake these cookies?"
 Iva Crouse, 85, White County

We had to get sugar stamps, but you just didn't get sugar. We got molasses out at Aberdeen. It was called New South, from New Orleans. I got a half gallon a week, and that was what we used for sweetening.
 Eunice Houze, 75, Ohio County

Sugar was rationed. As a substitute, we planted cane. We would "top" the cane when it was ready for harvest. We hauled it into the yard at night, by lantern light, and sometimes by moonlight. We would strip the blades off the stalk.
 Then in the morning we would load them on the one-horse wagon and take it to the sorghum mill. The juice was pressed out by horse-power. The juice ran into a pan, was boiled down to a syrup which we used for sweetening and on hot biscuits, also to make cakes and cookies.
 Murriel Sisson, 75, Brown County

We used a great deal of rice and potatoes and beans for food. Fresh fruits and vegetables were in very short supply.

Mary Graver, 81, Wayne County

'Course, we was on the farm, we raised an awful lot of our own. Potatoes, cabbages and everything like that. And, yes, we canned a lot.

Maggie Owen, 95, Whitley County

INFLUENZA EPIDEMIC

Another thing connected with World War I was the terrible epidemic of flu, influenza, that seemed to be connected with the servicemen.

Schools were closed, churches were closed, all entertainment houses, like movies, were closed for weeks at a time, and there were many casualties.

This was such a severe form of influenza that some people's health was damaged for the rest of their lives, because of heart trouble and respiratory diseases.

Mary Graver, 81, Wayne County

Horace was in the service. He was only in three months. He was taken during the flu epidemic, and during that time he didn't do anything except help take care of the flu patients. A couple of times he came home with one of the Richmond boys who had died. They sent the body back, and somebody came with them.

He had saved about $90 and he put it in savings before he went, and when he got there he didn't have any money. Their uniforms weren't issued because they were so busy taking care of the sick, and he didn't have enough clothes, so he had to buy some. I have always kidded him about this, so I sent him money. I imagine the amount wasn't very big, but he would always say, "Well, Donna kept me while I was in the service."

You were talking about the flu epidemic. How did this affect you?

We had it around here, but I don't remember any deaths in Richmond. It was so prevalent in those camps. I guess that's where our minds were, well, at least that's where mine was. No one in our family had it.

Donna Parker, 83, Wayne County

Toward the end, my youngest brother was in the navy and my oldest brother was in the next draft, so my brother in Detroit came home.

And then they had flu, and my sister and I and my father had all the work to do. My mother was in Pennsylvania 'cause her father was sick, and we three had all the work to do. There was a whole family in the neighborhood that had flu. My sister and I'd ride horseback over there and help out.

Grace Heinzman, 86, Hamilton County

During WW I all the boys died with flu and everybody else all over the country. It was terrible. Nobody met, and you just stayed home and taken care of things the best you could.

I know I had it. I was in terrible shape. Raymond and I both had it at the same time.

Vernell Saltzman, 81, Posey County

In 1918 we went through the flu epidemic. I'll never forget that, because the whole family came down with it, all except my brother just older than me. My grandmother from Boxley came over to care for us.

One evening she went out to feed the chickens and do the milking. She came back and couldn't find this brother that was the only one that wasn't sick. His name was Darrell, but she called him Durrell, and she ran all over the house, saying, "Durrell, Durrell, where are you?"

Well, we had a big old base burner in our living room. That's a big stove that burns hard coal. There would be red coals all the time, and it had isinglass doors all the way around so you could see the fire.

Well, she finally looked up, and there sat my brother on top of this stove, clear up on the very top, shivering like a leaf. She said, "Durrell, you've got the flu." And down he came and went to bed.

So we finally all had the flu. Our neighbors were dying, some of them, and each neighbor would try to go help the other one out.

Beulah Grinstead, 68, Hamilton County

During the flu epidemic of 1918, my mother got the flu. I will never forget that. She was upstairs in the bedroom. My dad had some queer ideas about health, and he had them until his dying day. That is, when you are sick, you go to bed and you don't eat. You fast completely. Although he said it was all right for mother to have some fruit. So he bought some grapefruit. In those days you didn't have fruit on hand very often, so that was a special treat. So we girls thought, "Can we have some of that?" Our mother would sneak us a bite once in a while.

So Mother was in bed then during that flu period. My dad also believed in having you perspire. He'd wrap you in wet towels and then wrap you in blankets. She survived all that, and none of the rest of us took it.

Inez Walther, 70, Jasper County

In 1918-1919 there was a flu epidemic.

Yes, we all had the flu that winter, and, oh, that was terrible! There were six of us, and I don't remember how many was in bed at one time with it, about half, I suppose, at one time. I never will forget that.

Did you have medications, or did they keep you in bed, or did the doctor come to the house?

Oh, we stayed in bed. Yes, he came to see us, but we stayed in bed mostly. I know all during that winter, somebody was in bed about all winter.

And the old house we had moved in wasn't too nice, either, and Mom papered that living room with newspaper. And we would lay there in bed and we tried to see what we could read in those newspapers. That helped us to read better. And, as far as papering, what was the difference if it was newspaper or fancy flowered paper? It was nice and clean. It answered the purpose.

Laura Drake, 72, Parke County

At our house, peppermint was good for anything. You took a spoonful of sugar and put a few drops of peppermint on it, and that was what was used.

When the flu was so bad when they had the flu epidemic, we were all sick but my dad. Dad was the only one that was up, and that was when peppermint was really used then.

Ellen McAfee, 68, Marshall County

I can remember during World War I when they had that flu epidemic, my mother would use an asafetida bag. I don't know whether you know that stuff.

I've heard about it, but I don't know much about it.

She put it in a little cloth bag and tied with a string and put it around our necks, and she declares this is the reason we didn't have the flu.

We continued going to school. I remember one day there was only two in the second grade that was there at school, so they dismissed school for a while, because there was so many out with flu.

Alice Guyer, 68, Wabash County

Did you have the flu in 1918?

Yes, we had the flu. The flu was so bad that people couldn't get help. I thought I'd go to a neighbor and try to help them. I went and was there one day, and I took the flu and had to go home.

They said afterwards, the doctor told us, if my mother went, she could have taken care of them, because she wouldn't have taken the flu. She had the flu when I was about fifteen or sixteen. We called it the grippe then, and she had it pretty bad. I guess that sort of immunized her.

Grace Elrod, 86, Jasper County

Our oldest boy just lived eight weeks. This was the year this flu was so bad. And my brother was moving, and they came down here, and they had the flu. Then the baby got the flu, and he was just eight weeks old when he died.

Pearl Garrison, 92, Carroll County

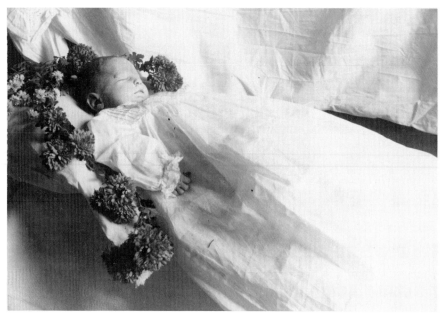

A dead baby laid out at home. Pictures such as these were often taken when the family had no other photograph of the child.
Submitted by Rush County

I am the oldest of the family and I have a sister five years younger than me. A little baby was born when I was ten, during the influenza epidemic in 1918. Our mother almost didn't live, and the baby didn't live.

I remember coming home. I knew there was a baby, because I had looked in the dresser drawers and saw the pretty outing flannel things with crocheted edges, and I knew there was a baby [coming] but they didn't tell the children then.

When I came home one evening, there was my father with this tiny, tiny baby, trying to feed it with a medicine dropper, and Dad wouldn't let me see my mother.

My sister was up at the neighbors. Grandmother told me to do my chores. I had rabbits to feed and chickens to tend.

When I came in, the baby wasn't in the room. I looked in the front room, and the little baby was on a blanket on the piano bench. I started to weep, and Grandmother said, "Don't you let out one tiny yelp. Your mother is so sick. You'll make her more sick than she is!" I hightailed it out of there.

Ilo Coffing, 76, Cass County

ARMISTICE DAY

I can remember the day the Armistice was signed. The whole school went upstairs, in the old school building, and we sang all the war songs that we could think of. Many of them you don't hear anymore. It was such songs as "Over There," "Keep the Home Fires Burning," "There's a Rose that Grows in No Man's Land," and "Katy." There was a lot of them, and we sang them all. We sang all that morning.

That's very fresh in my memory. I was, I believe, in the fourth grade at that time.

Ada Clarkson, 71, Jennings County

On Armistice Day, someone telephoned [that] they were having parades in town, so we thought that would be a good day just to go to town and see things. We thought we'd take the eggs in, but the stores were all closed, and people were tooting their horns and yelling. It just seemed like, sort of silly. So that was what Armistice Day meant to me. I thought, well, some of the boys I knew at the Grange and the neighborhood would be coming back in a few weeks, but it took months till they came back.

Grace Heinzman, 86, Hamilton County

One of my best memories of that time was when the war ended. I got to go into town, and we just danced all over town that night. I wasn't allowed to dance, because my parents didn't approve of dancing, but the snake dance was different. You just put your hands on the shoulders of the one in front of you. I expect there was a mile of us going around town that night, up one street and down another, singing and yelling and carrying on, because the war had ended.

Beulah Mardis, 76, Johnson County

Did you tell me your husband was in the first World War?

Yes, we were married after he came back. You know, he came back and he said, "The country will never be the same." The boys were rowdy, drinking, smoking, and their morals were breaking down, and he thought that the country would never be the same.

And, you know, it has made changes from that time. Before World War I, things were repetitious. You did the same thing over and over, from one generation to the next. There wasn't the progress that we have today. Things have moved fast in my lifetime.

Alma Knecht, 78, Wabash County

THE TWENTIES

In bloomers and middy blouse, this
fashionable young lady is ready for a
"spin" in her car.
Submitted by Starke County

What kind of clothes did people wear in the early '20s?

They wore long dresses, I know, they was ankle length. We wore a lot of long dresses early in the '20s. Suits—a lot of suits those days. We wore a lot of woolen stuff them days.

Also, there were a lot of gay times in those times. The music was quite gay and things like that. What kinds of music did you know about?

Violins. Homer Fox and all the neighbor men those days played violins, and we had square dances. We'd go around to the homes of us young couples, and they'd have square dances and Homer Fox and other men would play the violins.

Wouldn't a house be rather small for square dances?

That's where we had 'em. I cleared out a front bedroom and it would make it big enough. You'd have to take the beds out, and take the carpet up. You couldn't square dance with carpet on the floor. We went around to all the homes.

How many couples would there be at a party?

Oh, six or eight, something like that. But usually they'd be about three or four at a time that would square dance—about four couples. Two sets took two couples. They'd make two sets, and we'd dance about two or three dances, and then they would quit and let some of the rest of 'em dance.

The 1920s was noted for getting so many people to smoke. What about that?

I never smoked, but Fred would smoke a cigar once in a while. He said he didn't know where they get any kick out of a cigarette, but he smoked a cigar.

Drinking came in a great deal then.

Yes, it did, but that didn't bother us.

When did you have your first automobile?

Well, it was a Model T. It was after we had been married about three or four years, in the early 1920s. We went with a horse and buggy, and then we got a Model T.

Trilla Alderson, 83, Vermillion County

What about smoking in the '20s?

I wasn't exposed to it by any of our family. One thing was a fact, though, if a woman smoked, it really downgraded her.

Gladys Tribolet, 71, Huntington County

In the 1920s you would have been just a teenager. Do you remember about folks drinking, smoking or any of those things?

Oh, yes, I knew about those things.

My grandmother, my mother and my aunt thought that cards were a device of the devil. They did *not* play cards, but, oh, you should have seen them play dominoes. Now what is the difference?

Ilo Coffing, 75, Cass County

Skirts went up and hair was bobbed.
Note the mandolin.
Submitted by Rush County

Dresses changed quite a bit in the '20s. How did you react to it?

I guess we went along with the trends as much as we could. We re-modeled our dresses as best as possible.

Otillia Buehler, 90, Dubois County

People always talk about the 1920s as being the Charleston and the wild era.

Yes, it was wild, all right! The girls wore their stockings rolled and everybody thought it was horrible.

And skirts came up.

Yes.

Camille Hey, 89, Shelby County

Women didn't bob their hair then [early 1900s], did they?

No. They put their hair up on their head with long braids.

They kind of followed the Bible verse, "The crowning glory of a woman is her hair," and they admired their hair and took care of it.

Yes. They wore long braids they wrapped around their head, and turned them up and then sometimes put a ribbon in the back.

That was a chore, taking care of all that hair, wasn't it? Did they have beauty shops then?

No. You just washed your own hair, and braided it yourself.

Francis Harley, 90, Marshall County

The women at that time, in the early part of the century, all wore their hair long. About the beginning of the 1920s they began to cut it and wear it bobbed. Most of them wore it straight, hanging down just below their ears.

I would have liked to cut my hair, but my mother didn't want me to. Of course, I was in my twenties and could have done what I wanted, but I always tried to please my mother, so I didn't cut my hair.

I went to Ball State Teacher's College, and everybody was getting their hair cut. So, finally, my mother told me that I could cut mine if I wanted to. So I had it cut right away, and I have worn it short ever since.

Ruth Snyder, 83, Marshall County

Oh, that brings up a very unhappy day. I had a lot of hair. Braids, big braids all around my head. When I had my hair cut and went home, my baby, who was about nine months old, wouldn't even come to me. But, after a while, she decided it was Mom after all. So we got together again, in a few minutes.

Mildred McCay, 85, Tippecanoe County

In the '20s, I've heard it said, that women wore short skirts and cut off their hair. Were you involved in any of this?

My skirts weren't too short, but I did have my hair cut for the first time in a barbershop.

I know my husband didn't like me with short hair, and he was very profound in saying so. In fact, when I went home with short hair, he didn't have very much to say for two or three days.

You are saying that you had your hair cut without his permission?
I didn't think it was necessary to ask his permission.
Mary Graver, 80, Wayne County

I got my hair bobbed after I was married. That was the big thing to do. I didn't like it, after I had it cut off.

Did you save your hair?
Yes, I saved my hair, and I got it somewhere at home yet.

Did your husband want you to have it bobbed?
Oh, he thought it was fine.

He was more in favor than you were?
Yes, he was. His niece dressed it, after I was so discouraged with it. She had a beauty shop, and she dressed it for me. It sure felt different, after having it long so long.
Camille Hey, 89, Shelby County

I remember the first beauty shop. That was after the children were grown, that I went to the first beauty shop. They had that great big old iron thing that they put on your head all over [for a permanent wave]. I don't know what kind of a thing it was; anyway, you couldn't move around under it if you wanted to.

You looked like a monster with that on, didn't you?
Yes, they would wrap your hair around it and then turn on the heat, and you just sat there. That was heavy.
Francis Harley, 90, Marshall County

I remember during prohibition, we'd be in bed at night, or in the house, and a car would go by real fast—I suppose forty miles an hour at that time. And Mother would say, "Maybe it's a rum rider," and I'm sure that had to do with prohibition. Somebody was taking whiskey someplace, because it was always at night that she'd mention that.
Evelyn Rigsby, 58, Madison County

What do you remember about prohibition and bootlegging?
Well, down around Mansfield there was a place where they made liquor and sold it. They said that somebody down there made it, BUT I DIDN'T GO DOWN THERE! HA!

I was just wondering if it did occur in this area?
Yes, it did. That's what they said, but I didn't investigate.
Hazel Thomas, 81, Parke County

What about drinking in the '20s?

They had what they called roadhouses, and you could buy liquor that was homemade. People went in there and had their parties, and a lot of them were raided, with arrests being made.

Did people get sick from this?

Yes, they had a lot of what they called rotten liquor, and some would just get deathly sick from it.

Gladys Tribolet, 71, Huntington County

[Editor's note: The women have many recollections of the Ku Klux Klan for two reasons. The first reason is that one of the topics of the interviews was a specific question on the Ku Klux Klan. However, the second reason is that the Klan was very active in Indiana through this period, and almost everyone had at least some knowledge of its activities.]

Did you ever hear of the Ku Klux Klan?

Yes, I saw a cross burned one time. There was an awful crowd.

Did you have fear, seeing that cross? Did you understand what was going on?

I didn't understand what it was all about then, but I know Mom and Dad said, "That's too bad [that] something like that is happening."

Edna Maddox, 71, Grant County

I know there was an active Ku Klux Klan here in the county. I know they masked up and met at the Silver Creek Cemetery, once a month, I think.

Do you know of any orneriness they got into?

No, they didn't do anything. They just kept it social. And it didn't last too long.

Gleda Stevens, Union County

My brother-in-law was the head of it in the county there. And I recall two or three parades they had, but I never could thoroughly understand all about the Ku Klux Klan. It was kind of secretive, you know.

Edna Vandenbark, 91, Vanderburgh County

The main thing I remember was that it was quite a mystery. I was never quite sure, but I thought I had two uncles in it—one from my mother's family and one from my father's. I never asked and I never knew for sure.

Ruth Bateman, 76, Daviess County

I never did know for sure, but the first place that I worked, I thought the man that owned the business belonged, and that they had meetings there.

They would always send me somewhere else while they were having their meetings. He also received a lot of Ku Klux Klan mail, catalogs with their uniforms in it, letters and such; yet he claimed that he didn't belong.

That kind of scared me.

Evelyn Buchanan, 78, Scott County

Three women and one man pose with their banner for the Women's Ku Klux Klan No. 93 of Hartford City.
Cecil Beeson Collection
Courtesy Indiana Historical Society

I can remember they had a march in a neighboring town. My mother and father and another couple of friends of theirs went. We were parked along the side of the street, and we saw them march down the street.

My mother and father thought that was just awful, but to me, I just didn't understand what it was.

Verlee Jochum, 64, Dubois County

Just about half or more of the people in Parke County belonged to it. I didn't, nor Joe didn't and Joe's mother didn't.

I couldn't see where they could be Christians if they hated certain people. But they pretended to be Christians and held [some] of their meetings in churches. Preachers preached that, you know, that you should join the Ku Klux Klan. They had church meetings and filled the churches, and took up money. They passed the plate around and took in a lot of money, which probably went to the head, to the upper officers.

I thought they did a lot of damage. They burned a cross in the courthouse yard for a certain woman who lived right there, a Catholic woman. I like that woman, and I thought they weren't much of a Christian if they could do that.

Hazel Thomas, 81, Parke County

Oh, yes, when we lived in Bridgeport, nearly everybody down there belonged to it. It was a big organization. I don't know if they done any harm or nothing. They were just so strict against so many things. I didn't approve of it.

I don't think they done too much there. Oh, they had their meetings, burnt their crosses and all of that. But I don't remember any killing or nothin'.

Hazel Dolkey, 79, Knox County

Well, all I remember were the sheets over their head were all white, and they had a place for their eyes out. Then they burned a fiery cross, and everybody was afraid of the Ku Klux Klan when they burned crosses and done things.

Do you know why they burned crosses?

No, I don't. I think it was to scare people, colored and white people, too.

Francis Harley, 90, Marshall County

Were there blacks in the neighborhood that they wanted to frighten away?

No, I don't think so, because there weren't any blacks around here that I know of.

You don't know what their objectives were here?

No, but I think my dad belonged to it.

Icil Hughes, 78, Grant County

I was in a school play, and my dad would take me into practice. We came home one night— we drove a horse and buggy, of course—no car, as yet, or not too many.

When he went to put the horse away in the barn, all the other horses were loose. Some of them had part of the manger hanging to them, and some had broke their tie straps. Dad couldn't figure out what in the world it was.

So when we went to the house, my sister and mother told us that someone had burnt a cross out on the road. And before they lit the cross, they had set off a big burst of dynamite, and that evidently was what had frightened the horses.

The next morning, we all went out there, and, sure enough, out on the other side of the road—Dad had left his disk there—and they had fastened the cross to the disk, and had burnt the tongue out of the disk. The charred remains of the cross were there.

Then I remember a family coming down to the house across the street from the schoolhouse. I was in school, and all the schoolchildren were very interested in it. They had brought a brother-in-law down to be buried in the Butlerville Cemetery, and he was, or had been, a member of the Klan.

There was a large group of these white-robed people walking around and that interested the kids in school very, very much. We knew what it was, but that was about all.

Ada Clarkson, 70, Jennings County

One time we were traveling to Mishawaka and in the Mishawaka Hills was a Ku Klux Klan meeting. There was a large group of people gathered in white robes and hoods, and they were burning crosses in the hills.

One robed person was standing near the road, trying to get people to stop. I was pretty frightened.

Kathleen Blondia, 65, St. Joseph County

One time some of those hooded and draped men paraded in our church while we were having a meeting. I just vaguely remember that the door opened at the back, and about three of these people came in and stood at the front of the church. I don't know what was said; I just remember them coming in.

Was it scary?

Yes! Very much!

Alice Guyer, 68, Wabash County

I know that the Klan was active in this vicinity. I have heard my father say that, as a boy, he can recall the Klan coming one night and burning a cross in the field north of the house, which is the house where we now live.

I think he told me he was the most frightened that he had ever been, and that he hid under his uncle's bed. This probably would have that type of effect on a young person; it might even have that type of effect on someone not so young!

I recall my mother-in-law saying it was kind of an eerie feeling to know that some of your neighbors and relatives might even be involved with the Klan, but you never knew exactly who it was, because they were always disguised with their costuming. That there were people under there you should know, but you had no idea who it was. That would be kind of eerie.

Jane Gillooly, 37, Daviess County

I had an uncle that had quite a limp, and we had a lot of fun, because we knew he was walking past us, hopping along.

Gladys Tribolet, 71, Huntington County

They marched with their robes on. You would have to know these people to appreciate it, but Richard Vandivier's grandmother walked up to a man and she jerked his hood up, and she said, "Now, Frank, anybody would know you by your big feet." It was a wonder somebody hadn't assaulted her; you weren't supposed to say anything to them.

Now my dad was what you would call conservative, and the ones that we did know that were in [the Klan], we weren't around much. We just went to church things.

But I can remember Richard Vandivier's grandmother, "Well, Frank, anyone would know your big feet." He had a white sheet on. It must have taken a double bed size to fit him.

Elsie Canary, 79, Johnson County

My parents never thought very much of them [Klan]. We lived close to Wanamaker, and they were active in and around that community; but we were never allowed to go, and my father and brother never went either, so I really didn't know much about them.

But I can tell one funny little thing my husband told. He was a young man, probably still in high school, and his family had some land in different places, not real close to their farmhouse.

There was a group of Ku Klux Klan meeting at a little country church near Needham. It was quitting time, so my husband unhitched his horses and was going to drive them home. He was going to have to drive them through this group of Ku Klux Klan all dressed up in their whites.

There was devilment in him, so he wound the lines around the collars of the horses and smacked the horses on the rear, and turned them loose. Of course, they were anxious to get home, and they run right through the Ku Klux Klan. Those Klanners all run and tried to climb fences and everything else.

He loves to tell that story. He was Catholic, and the church was within a half mile of their house. It was sort of a get-even deal, I think.

Opal Gallagher, 72, Shelby County

I can remember the days of the Ku Klux Klan very well. I was in Indianapolis teaching school at that time, and I can remember the stories of the fiery crosses and the state leader (I guess that was what his official title was)—I'm not going to mention his name.

While I was there in Indianapolis, he was tried for murdering some woman that he had coaxed into going up to Chicago with him as a secretary and instead it was for other purposes, and he was convicted of this murder.

He spent a great number of years in prison, and finally he was paroled, but he had to leave the country and go someplace else and live.

I guess that put kind of a damper on the Ku Klux Klan here in Indiana. I remember the first two or three years I was in Indianapolis, the papers were just full of that.

Ruth Snyder, 83, Marshall County

I think I had neighbors that were in the Ku Klux Klan, but that was a very secret organization.

Now there was an organization called the Horse Thief Detection Association. I don't know much about it, only those things were kept pretty secret, because if you stole a horse, you were in pretty bad trouble.

Ruth Dane, 81, Madison County

In about 1920 there was a little Ku Klux Klan activity in Perry County, but not much, I think. The biggest target of the Klan was the colored people, and there were very few colored people in the county, so they didn't have much to fuss about.

But we did have what they called White Caps in the neighborhood, that operated about like the Klan. They were secret, and went with their faces covered and a white robe.

They tried to scare people, and if they had a grudge against someone, or thought he was lazy and not providing for his family, they'd take him out and flog him. [They'd] leave a bunch of switches at people's door as a warning.

But what broke it up (I've been told this), was, one night they went to one man's house where he had already gone to bed. No one locked their doors, so they walked right in and was going to take him out.

His wife picked up a chopping axe by the door and buried it in someone's back. They took the hurt fellow and left ahead of time, and that was the end of the White Caps.

Nellie Frakes, 71, Perry County

I don't remember the Ku Klux Klan from the 1920s, but last year we were down in Nashville, Tennessee, and the Ku Klux Klan was standing on the corners down there, trying to collect money for their causes.

And the police were standing right there close to them, so that they wouldn't hassle the people while they were there.

But, I don't know just how to describe it. It gave you kind of a scary feeling. They had their white outfits on down there. That's the first time I'd ever come in contact with anything like that, but it kind of gave you a weird feeling when you see them all dressed up. Oh, I don't know!!

LaVerda Shearer, 56, Whitley County

THE GREAT
DEPRESSION

The huckster wagon brought groceries to
the farm family in this 1930s shot. Note
that the driver is weighing a live chicken,
which will be used to pay the grocery bill.
J. C. Allen Collection

Tell me about the Great Depression and the 1930s and how it affected you, your family and your neighbors and friends.

Well, that was something terrible. Everybody was going along good and here the Depression came. Prices went way down. All of our farm prices down so low. We had a lot of hogs and cattle to sell, but the price on the grain was way down. And people was just heartsick about it. They couldn't make enough to hardly pay their taxes.

Well, a lot of them just didn't have enough to eat, and they had to go down to the trustee and he would give them money to hold them over until they got some things.

But out in the country here, eggs was only eight cents a dozen and milk was eight cents a gallon, and corn was twenty cents [a bushel] and oats was eights cents a bushel. You could sell the stuff, but it didn't bring you enough to keep a-goin'.

Lots of time we'd get a bunch of cornmeal ground up so we could give it to a lot of our friends and they'd make mush out of that. I told my husband, I said, "I know a lot of our good friends that don't have nothing to eat hardly, and they've got kids, and we're going to give them eggs." I said, "I don't care about selling the eggs at eight cents a dozen."

We had plenty of everything. We had all we needed to eat. We had all that kind of stuff. And, as far as the Depression, it didn't hurt us too much, only when the banks went closed. That was really a blow. Your money was in there, and the banks was closed, and you couldn't get it out.

We had money enough to build our new home, and the banks were all closed. You couldn't get anything out. Well, I was heartsick, of course. I had to take a good bawl. You know, if you can't get over anything , and can't shake it, well, you just bawl and you think, "Well, that will help."

My husband told me, he says, "Cut out your worrying. We're young, and we're healthy, and we'll make enough money and then we can build a house when we have enough money saved up." We lost $6,000, which was what we was going to put in the house.

So, when we'd sell cattle and things like that, we buried our money, and, by gosh, that was a good place for it—under the ground. When we got ready to build, when we paid off the lumber and everything, they begin to laugh. They said, "Where you had this money? It's all mildewed." I said, "That's not mildewed. That's ground. That's good earth."

So everybody was happy when things picked up. My husband was laid off at the time. He worked at Orton's, but he was laid off. Well, all of them was laid off. They just didn't have anything—no jobs or anything—for them. So we was just about closed down all the way around. But everybody sure was glad when things started picking up, and they could sell their stuff.

How much was the land worth then?

Oh, it was around $80 to $100 an acre, and then when things got better and picked up, why, it came on up to $200 to $300. And look at it now. My land, it's just went crazy. Ground from $2,000 to $3,000, and some of it even $4,000 an acre.

Tell me some more about the Depression and hard times.

During this here hard time, they was people who'd go around and steal. You wouldn't even know they was going to be around, and the next thing you know, here they was, stealing your chickens or your cattle and things like that.

We had a neighbor down the way, and they had full-blooded cattle and had them out in the pasture. One night there was somebody come out there and they killed one of their young heifers that was going to have a calf. They shot her with darts, so there would be no gun noise.

They butchered her. They took the two hind legs and the front legs and the next morning when they went out to feed their cattle, there lay this nice heifer that had been killed, and she had had a little heifer calf in her. They said they was just heartsick, because she was such a wonderful cow, and somebody would come out there and kill their cattle right out in their barnyard and steal them, and they didn't know it until the next day.

And there was also something that don't sound like it would have amounted to much, but it did to these people. They had an old hen a-setting and there was a funeral in the neighborhood. This guy came out, and he stole a whole bunch of this old lady's chickens, and he even took the setting hen off the eggs they was going to hatch the next week. So that was the end of her little chickens right there.

And this here neighbor that had her chickens stole, she came down and told us about it, and she just cried. She said, "I'm just so poor and hard up and to think somebody would come and steal my chickens like that while I'd been gone to a funeral."

Well, this guy happened to tell my husband. He said, "We're just so hard up we don't hardly have nothing to eat," and he told how he would go out in the country whenever he'd read in the paper there was a funeral. Then he would go out and steal a bunch of chickens, and that's what they would have to live on.

So, that was Depression for the people in town, that they stole off the country folks. And the country folks had worked like the dickens to get these things, and that's the way they'd do. And they'd even come and steal hogs. You just about had to lock your fences, and then they would saw the locks off, so they could get your things.

It wasn't safe to go away on a Sunday, 'cause when you'd come back, a lot of times all your stuff would be gathered up out of your garden. All your cabbage, tomatoes, and everything like that. A lot of times we'd go away and when we'd come back that evening, why our garden products would be all gone.

Masa Scheerer, 82, Huntington County

What was life like then? Can you remember?

Oh, yes, I should say! I made clothes for them girls, out of clothes that was give to me. I made them even coats, and I made the boys overalls and shirts.

Yes, I should say I do remember. Workin' for a dollar a day, that didn't go very far.

Did you have a garden?

Oh, yes, we had a garden, and we raised hogs and we raised chickens and had cows, and we sold milk. We didn't go hungry, we always had our own meat and eggs and milk.

And then when the children got big enough to work; the boys, the farmers around in the summertime would have them to work for 'em. Then the girls, they worked for a lady up here in town when she needed help. And they all knowed how to work.

How about the young people today? Do you see a great difference?

Oh, yes, my goodness! 'Course we lived down in there where they couldn't go a lot like they do now. They wasn't on the road half the time. They made their own entertainment with the neighbors, close neighbors. Oh, it's a lot different now.

Do you think it was better?

I sure do! It was better in lots of ways.

Pearl Kincaid, 79, Owen County

DEPRESSION ON THE FARM

The Depression didn't hit us when they say now, when the stock market crashed in 1929. That wasn't when the Depression hit us in the country, as much as in the '30s.

Catherine Summers, 67, Harrison County

What effect did the Depression have on your family?

Since we were farmers, it didn't affect us too much. We had plenty to eat, but we had no money to buy anything. We took our eggs and cream to the local grocery store and traded it for groceries. Our chicken feed came in colorful sacks, so we made our clothing out of the feed sacks. We also made bed sheets and towels out of the feed sacks. The men cut the wood for our fuel, because that's the only thing we burned then, was wood.

We did have neighborhood gatherings. We would get together in the evening and have parties. Church was our greatest recreation, activities from the church. We had Sunday School parties and that kind of thing.

Mary Dean, 76, Clinton County

Outside of just not having ready cash, it didn't affect the people that lived on the farms like it did the people in town. It was bad for people that had been used to a lot of money, because they didn't know how to do without.

We got along very well.

Zelma Blocher, 81, Scott County

What do you remember of the Depression?
It didn't affect us much. It was like one of my cousins said, "We never had anything, so we couldn't have any less."

We never had any money to spend. My folks had bought this farm, and the money they could possibly get together, had to go to pay the payments. They were so frugal and saving to get the money to pay on that note, that we never had a lot of things. I never had a ready-made dress. We never went to a show. There just wasn't money spent.

So we really didn't feel much difference. My parents may have had a lot of worries about getting the money to pay the taxes, but I would say that that was the only way the Depression affected us.

Beulah Mardis, 76, Johnson County

At the time you were married, were times easy then?
No, it was right during the Depression. Of course, living on a farm at that time, you always raised what you had and canned everything, and you didn't buy everything like you do now. You had your eggs and milk and things. You had your meat, that was very good.

People who worked in the factories had a lot harder time than the ones who lived on farms, because you could raise your own food.

However, it was hard, because you didn't get very much for what you did raise. You didn't get much money for it. Lots of times grocery stores would trade your milk and eggs for things you needed.

The banks were closed, so what money you had in the bank, you couldn't get it. It was hard, but we got through. You just raised what you could and did the best you could.

Elma Matthew, 75, Madison County

Before times had gotten hard, he [husband] had gotten registered
Jersey cows and bought a new automobile and a new tractor. And then
things went down, and it was hard to make payments on things.

Hogs sold cheap and the price of milk went down. In fact, we knew
of one family that had some sheep to send in [to market]. So, when
somebody was taking a load of livestock to Cincinnati, they sent one
of their sheep to sell. They got a bill back for five cents. It didn't bring
enough to pay the cost of the trucking.

Thelma Nixon, 67, Union County

It was terrible. We could hardly live. We sold hogs for 2¢ a
pound, and corn for 10¢ a bushel. One year, if we had sold everything
we had, it wouldn't have paid the taxes.

Myrtle Fisher, 88, Parke County

**How about raising and selling a crop of tobacco? What did that
average?**

Three or four cents about that time. I just don't know how people
did.

Eunice Houze, 75, Ohio County

Eggs sold for $2.10 to $2.15 a case, which was 30 dozen eggs. We
sold cream for around $2.00 to $2.15. We had 200 hogs that we sold
for 3¢ a pound. They said they were a little bit overweight, was the reason they sold so cheap, but after we made the trade on them, they sold
for more. We bought 2,000 bushels of corn for 25¢ a bushel when we
moved to this place, and we sold our corn that we had at home for the
same price.

Margaret Dean, 77, Scott County

One year, I remember, it was a drought, and the corn was just a little
over a yard high. You cut the stalk with no corn hardly on it. It was
mostly little nubbins and just stalk. So you didn't have no corn to feed
the hogs either. The hogs were only 2¢ a pound, and the most you used
to get out of a cow was fifty dollars.

But then stuff was all cheaper those days, too. Ten pounds of sugar
for 50¢ and a great big sack of 24 pounds of flour for 50¢.

Francis Harley, 90, Marshall County

I know one year we had such an early frost that our corn didn't
mature, so we used that for fuel in our heating stove.

Iva Crouse, 85, White County

You were talking about a year when it was dry and there was not much of a crop. Was that during the Depression?

Yes, it was during the Depression. It was in '34-'35. That was the year that we put out pickles, and we had to dress the kids on the pickle money. We had to depend on that, because milk was no price, and the pasture dried up, and we didn't raise any crops. That was really the worst we went through.

How many years were there?

There was a couple of years, but it seemed longer.

Bessie Werner, 80, Pulaski County

NO MONEY

The Depression, that was quite a hard time. Everyone our age remembers it. We didn't have, and we didn't know what it was to have. If you had a nickel, you were pretty proud.

Pearl Snider, 70, Ripley County

We talk about the Depression sometimes. We had a man work for us and when Saturday night came, we would give him what money we had and then a basket of eggs (you could take your eggs to the grocery and exchange them), and we stayed home. Oscar had the eggs and the money, which wasn't much. I'm not begrudging him, but we just didn't have anything left.

Elsie Canary, 79, Johnson County

During the Depression, my dad walked from our house to the Fireproof Door. He saved the gasoline so we could go to church on Sunday.

How far would this have been?

Four or five miles, and he never missed a day of work, either.

Even when it was cold, or snowed?

They didn't have snow days in those days.

Helen Sauser, 64, Wayne County

We didn't think we had money to buy license plates for our old Model T we drove, so my dad and my husband, they took old plates and painted over them the color they had come out with that year. Of course, we drove over country roads with them and got dirt on them, and they got by for a whole year with homemade licenses.

Pearl Sollars, 70, Tippecanoe County

A friend sold us a lot. He really gave it to us. We just paid the back taxes and assessments on it.

Mable Hunter, 70, Jasper County

The Depression was awful. You didn't have enough money to pay taxes, and you had to go borrow it and when it came time to pay that, you had to borrow again. It was terrible.

We didn't have no money. If I was a-going' to town, my husband would reach down and get his pocketbook and say, "You're welcome to any, if I got any."

Flossie Foster, 95, Hendricks County

You had to limit your spending, didn't you?

You sure did. You just had so much. And one night, I'll never forget, we always saved money back to buy gas out here at Hicks'. And Carl, he hadn't got to stay in town as long as he wanted to. He was just a little fellow, and he was cross and kind of crying; so when he got in the car, I said, "Here, you can hold the dollar." That kind of pleased him, I guess.

But, anyhow, we got out there at Hicks', he didn't have the dollar. And I said, "What did you do with that dollar?" "Oh," he said, "I dropped it back there." And I said, "Where did you drop it?" "Well, back there by the church," he said. So we went back, and, sure enough, we found that dollar.

How much gas would it buy, do you remember?

I don't remember exactly, but a dollar would buy a lot then.

Bertha Pampel, 83, Benton County

You were married about the time of the Depression. Tell me, did it make a difference in your income?

Oh, yes, we didn't have any income (laughter).

How did you manage?

Oh, he did get a few jobs, but not many. We didn't lose our home, like a lot of people did. They came out with a new kind of government loan, that reduced the payments down to about ten dollars a month, which we could meet. He managed to work enough so that we could make those payments. If it hadn't been for that, we'd have lost our home.

Many others right around us did, but we didn't. We managed to get ten dollars from someplace, don't ask me how.

But we were lucky, one of the lucky ones.

Alma Smith, 73, Grant County

I was married in 1930 and I went out on the farm, and that was a bad year for farmers, so we really had to be saving. We were buying the farm, and I can remember two different times when we didn't have enough money to make the payment; we had to make it at two different times. We paid what we could then, and in a few months, when we got some more money, we made the other payment.

Ruby Leedy, 76, Whitley County

We lost our home out on Oak Hill during the Depression. [There was] no work, and my husband was laid off. He finally worked out east of town for 90 days for a dollar a day and his dinner.

Lulu Graves, 92, Marshall County

I lived through the Great Depression. I'll never forget it. During the late '20s and early '30s, I went to high school day after day when my daddy did not have a penny to give me to buy a penny pencil.

The Depression took my daddy's farm. He moved in November of my senior year in high school.

Beulah Mardis, 68, Hamilton County

GETTING CASH MONEY

If we needed something for school, or if we needed a new pair of shoes or clothes, we'd help sack up wheat. I can remember, many a times, that my sister and I helped sack up wheat, and Dad would take it to town.

I know we would have ten sacks of wheat, and that would probably be two bushels in a sack, and my sister and I would get a new pair of shoes. That would be about what they would cost, would be what the wheat would bring.

Alma Small, 61, Dubois County

We cracked hickory nuts and took them to town. We made maple syrup and sold that. That is all the makings [for getting money] that we had to come out of the Depression.

Katharine Bothel, 53, Delaware County

Many times, if we needed some money, we'd gather up a few old hens and take them to town and sell them. We sold cream, and later on my husband started a dairy. For many years we had a dairy on the

farm. We delivered milk to a number of households and stores in all of
the surrounding towns.

   Emma Baker, 79, Scott County

   I remember one time, I wanted to go to see my folks. We didn't have
any money in the house to buy gasoline. We milked a lot of cows at
that time. I wanted to go, and Andy said maybe he could take what
cream we had and sell it in Connersville, because he had enough gas to
get to Connersville.

Counting eggs by "counts" with three in
each hand. Each count was a half dozen.
Unscrupulous egg buyers would sometimes
pick up four eggs in the less
conspicuous hand.
Purdue University

   So that's what we did. We took our cream and sold it in Connersville so we could get enough gas to get on out to see my parents and
then on back home again.

   Harriett Gwinnup, 73, Fayette County

I remember we had a little store and we served lunches. We served lunches to the men who worked on the WPA. I would fry thirty or forty pounds of fish and make them into fish sandwiches. We sold them for 15¢ a sandwich.

Hazel Clawson, 72, Benton County

We had chickens and I took eggs to town, and that was what I got my groceries with. I remember one time I took nine dozen to town, and it didn't buy a sack full.

My mother made butter and sold it. She had her own boxes, her butter boxes, made with her name on them. She would take it and deliver it to the homes. And that got to be too much of a pest, so she just took it to the grocery, and people came to the grocery and bought my Mom's butter.

Ruth Dye, 75, Martin County

We moved to town. He [husband] got work and he had work in the summer, and then in the winter he couldn't find anything.

We had one daughter, our youngest, was just a baby, and we had to buy milk for her, so I started baking cookies. And he peddled cookies all winter to make a living. He went door to door with a big basket. And we didn't have them in sacks, either, he just had the cookies on clean cloth in that basket.

You couldn't do that today.

Helen Shockey, 80, Grant County

We had to stay home many times, because we had no money to go anywhere.

Otillia Buehler, 90, Dubois County

At the time my brother was born, in '31, we didn't have any money, so to pay the doctor, they sold a cow. But we made it.

Catherine Summers, 67, Harrison County

I was in high school. I graduated in 1931. We tried so hard to get enough money so we could have a school yearbook. We sold newspapers, magazines, anything we could get our hands on, to get enough money, but we failed.

We had our 50th reunion in 1981. Quite a few of our boys and girls talked things over, and we said we thought that's why our class had always seemed a little closer together, because we went through so much in the Depression.

Gaby Moon, 70, Clay County

When I graduated from high school, there was absolutely no money. My class had money in the bank to put on the prom for the senior class. I was a junior when the bank folded, and there went our money! We couldn't get any money at all. The restaurant owner at Star City loaned us $10, and, believe it or not, we put on a prom for all the teachers, fifteen juniors and twenty-three seniors, all on that $10.

Mildred Weaver, 64, Pulaski County

Joe and I were farming, and money was so scarce, and we had this little girl. She came in 1930, and in 1931 we had lost a horse. We were still using horses, and we lost that horse, and money was so tight. We wondered where we were ever going to get enough money to buy another horse.

We searched around, and we found one. Lloyd Conrad had one that we bought, and he said, "Joe, you don't need to pay for it all at once. Just pay as you can."

But it was in our mind that that was a debt that should be paid. Then it came time to buy the seed corn, and time to plant oats, and you needed fertilizer. Joe had a Ford tractor, and you needed fuel and oil for that.

Joe sold a whole load of oats to buy a tank of gasoline. I don't remember how much oats was—maybe a few cents a bushel, but we often talked about how it took a load of oats to buy a tank of gasoline for the tractor.

Alma Knecht, 78, Wabash County

My daddy took out a life insurance policy when I was first born. It matured and they hadn't cashed it in. They needed a new roof on the barn, so they cashed it in and put a new roof on the barn.

Cledia Bertke, 55, Perry County

EMPLOYMENT DURING THE
DEPRESSION—MEN

What effect did the Depression have on you?

Terrible. We had to give up our first home, and my husband was forced to go into business for himself and work for practically nothing—I mean nothing. It left a scar I don't think we'll ever forget.

Marie Unfried, 71, Vanderburgh County

At the beginning of the Depression, my husband worked for a farmer over here close to Grange Corner. He worked for a dollar a day and took his own lunch, worked eight hours a day and walked, most of the time, to get over there. Our groceries usually ran around $3.00 a week. It was all we could spend.

Laura Drake, 72, Parke County

My husband worked on the Pennsylvania Railroad.

Was it steady work?

Yes, it was, but it got very bad when the Depression came. I remember the one check he got was for $1.68. He said, "If we didn't have to have a loaf of bread, I'd have it framed." But we had to spend it. But normally it was a good job. Paid about as good as any job at that time, I think.

Hope Kessler, 86, Allen County

You were an agricultural extension agent?

Yes, I graduated from Purdue in 1928, in the time of Depression and hard times. So I came back to my home farm in 1929 and was there until December of 1930, when I was elected county agent in Shelby County.

We had all of the bank failures, and I can remember in 1932 I was paid by Shelby County with IOU's, because the county did not have enough to pay their employees.

Wilbur Whitehead, 75, Boone County

We were married in the Depression, and it was difficult. My husband worked for 75¢ a day, and had a wife and baby.

Opal Gallagher, 72, Shelby County

We were pretty lucky through the Depression. My husband had a job all through.

Everybody else in the family didn't have none. So, each week, he would give each one of them two dollars a week, and they was tickled to death to get that two dollars. We tried to give to his brother, and my brother, the family, you know. My dad and mother, we was always trying to help them. Grandpa Dolkey, he had a job, but my dad didn't.

It was kind of hard for everybody, but we was lucky. We had a job.

Hazel Dolkey, 79, Knox County

EMPLOYMENT—WOMEN

I was working in a restaurant in 1932 or so, for $5 a week, seven days a week, ten hours a day, and walked three miles to work.

Now they get $5 an hour.

Achsa Nussbaum, 68, Benton County

High school was as far as I went, because I graduated in the middle of the Depression. I had to find a job and help my mother and dad live.

I got a job in an attorney's office and helped Mother and Daddy for several years before I got married. I worked for $15.00 a week, and thought it was a good salary.

Martha Whitehead, 72, Boone County

I remember the Depression. I just got out of nurse's training, and there wasn't any jobs. There was a need for it, but wasn't no money. I did a little private duty at $5.00 a day, and it was twenty-hour days in the hospital or at homes.

Mabel Bobbitt, 88, Shelby County

I worked for $3.00 a week. It was housework, and I got my food and lodging and three dollars money. That was in Elkhart, and then I would take a bus over the weekend home. It cost me 50¢ for that bus for a round trip to go from Elkhart to Nappanee.

Ellen McAfee, 68, Marshall County

What effect did the Depression have when you began as a home economics county agent here?

Well, our salary wasn't very high. I worked for $125.00 per month, plus 5¢ a mile for the miles I drove. So, really, that wasn't much money. We were expected to have a car, and we had to stay somewhere and eat all of our meals. We didn't have much left at the end of the time.

Alice Gentry, 68, Hamilton County

My mother took in washings and ironings and did house cleaning for people.

Jean Rechtenbaugh, 52, Marshall County

When I got out of school there wasn't any money to go to school further, and there weren't any jobs for girls or women, because there were so many men out of work, and they had to be served first.

My aunt and uncle owned the laundry. That was the first real job I had, working there at the laundry. And I hope I never come to that again. That's hard work.

Susie Burkhart, 67, Jackson County

We had an awful time through the Depression. Our children were growing up—we had some of them in college in the '30s. Our farm wasn't producing enough to keep us going. And before that we had lost two herds of milk cows—one with what they called Bang's disease and then one with tuberculosis. We depended on those cows for our expenses.

But we just kept trying and trying, and we kept our kids at school. At one time we thought we would lose our farm, because we couldn't pay what we owed on the mortgage and the interest, but we managed to come through. And saved the farm and got our kids all educated.

Did your husband ever work away from the farm?

Yes, when times were hard, he did. They had sunk a new mine just a little ways from us and he asked for a job and he worked there for fifteen years. And he worked there all during the Depression.

And you had boarders?

Oh, yes! One time there was a couple of men that stopped at our house, wanting to know if I could board them. They were helping sink that mine, and they lived up close to Greencastle, and they wanted to stay closer to the job.

Well, first I told then I couldn't do that. I did have an extra room upstairs, with two beds in it, but I had no way to heat it and I didn't have as much bedding as I needed.

Then I thought if I could keep them, that money would help us out. So I told them they could stay.

Well, when my husband came in and found out, he just hit the ceiling. That wouldn't do at all. I said that I had already told them that they could stay, and he'd have to tell them no, if he didn't want them.

So, he finally consented to have them stay. And before we knew it, there was another couple that wanted to stay, and so he told them they could (chuckle) after being so opposed to it. And you know, we kept on until they'd alternate beds. One couple worked at night would sleep in the daytime, and one that worked in the daytime would sleep at night, all in the same beds. So we got double out of that.

And you fed them all!

Yes, I fed them all. At one time I had nine men. And they must have been pretty good meals, because they'd go home and tell their families about what good food they had at our house (chuckles).

How much did they pay you to stay?

Let's see. The daily wage at the mine at that time was $3.65. And they each paid us that much for a week's board. By the time you multiply that by nine, why it helped us out a whole lot (chuckles). But it was a lot of work, it was a lot of hard work to it.

Ethel Downen, 95, Montgomery County

GOVERNMENT JOBS

My dad worked for the WPA. This was a type of welfare, but you had to work for your help. I think the WPA was a lot better than what they have today, and if I had anything to do with it, they'd have to work for welfare. There are many jobs they could do, instead of giving it [money] to them.

Kathleen Blondia, 69, St. Joseph County

I remember there was lots of people that was on that WPA. Roosevelt did that. It was simply to give jobs to the people that couldn't find jobs, and it was a government project.

They did all kinds of work. There's a lot of sidewalks—I think there's still some in Rockville—that had the initials on 'em, WPA. A lot of them around here worked on that.

And they worked on the road. In fact, they changed the road down east of us here from a crooked S curve to a straight hill. They kept them busy on the roads, ditches and things like that.

And that's also about the same time they had that CCC camp and I know they did a lot of work at Turkey Run [State Park]. All of their steps and a lot of the trails were made by the CCC boys.

This was the time President Roosevelt was instigating a lot of social programs. Do you know how they were received in this community?

They was really appreciated. That was their only means of living, was to have jobs like that.

Laura Drake, 72, Parke County

I was small, but I do remember the WPA. I know I would go somewhere, and I would see men leaning on their shovel handle. They weren't working so hard.

Cledia Bertke, 55, Perry County

Did you know anybody that worked in the WPA?

Yes, I had an uncle and a neighbor, too. This neighbor, he had a big family, but he was so proud he couldn't take it, and he finally quit. It embarrassed him so to have to work on the WPA.

Don't you feel that the WPA was the difference between starving?

Sure.

Do you feel like it was a really good program?

Sometimes I wonder if it wouldn't be better to put some of them on [now]. Make them get out and work for it. Clean up the roads like they did then, and the rivers, and the creeks. I don't know how much they worked, but they got a lot of clean-up work done.

Icil Hughes, 78, Grant County

It was a hard time for everyone. My dad was out of work for I don't know how many months. I don't remember whether it was during the middle '30s or early '30s, but the government came into Kokomo and had what they called a commissary. It was a big store building uptown where they had food and clothing and blankets and things, and my dad was lucky enough to get a job there. He got so much money a week, eight or ten dollars, and then he was allowed so many groceries, and that really helped out.

He would come home and tell us everyone he had seen up there getting what they called a county order. That was the welfare system in those days. We just couldn't believe some of the people we thought had plenty of money, but when the banks closed their doors, their money went with the bank. So they were up there, some of the wealthier people in town. Some of them would hang on to their automobiles, they just couldn't let go of their cars. They would have a maid or cook, and they would send the maid or cook around to this commissary to get their groceries and things for them. They would park about a block away; you got so you would know whose maids were coming in after groceries.

I know the government sent a bunch of blankets one time, pink and blue wool blankets. My older sister needed a coat and Mother made coats out of everything anybody would give her. All the relatives passed things around. So Dad came home with a couple of those blankets, blue ones. I don't know where the government got them, but the warehouse where they had had them had had a fire, and those blankets were kind of scorched around the edges. Mother took two of them and made my sister a coat, a pretty coat. But she [sister] said she never hated anything so much in her life as that old blue coat that was made from the government blankets.

Betty Alvey, 60, Howard County

DEPRESSION FINANCES

Now your husband was a pastor at this time?

Yes, and we had a little money in the bank. I don't remember, it seems like it was $150. We had two funerals that day, and we went to the first funeral and a man came up to me and he said, "Do you know the banks are going to close today?"

Well, I was going home between funerals. I didn't go to the cemetery with him. "Well, I will just walk uptown." We didn't live a block off Main Street. Now if you want to experience something, is to step up to that door, and it's locked, and you can't get in.

Your $150 was behind closed doors, locked doors.

That's right. They were locked, and you couldn't get in. Of course, a lot of people did have money. Well, this doctor, he had $10,000, and he took his gun and went down to the president of the bank, and he said, "You go in and get my $10,000." And he got it. But poor people didn't. The banks were just locked.

What did you live off of?

Well, of course, the people didn't have money to pay [us] either. Then a man came to our rescue, and gave us some money. But then, in time, like for the electric bill, they would take a check on what you had there in the bank. I think the first radio we had, we bought that way, because they would take a check on the bank, until we got our little bit of money out.

Audrey Blackburn, 86, Posey County

I think the worst thing that ever happened to us was when the First National Bank closed up. That made it real rough. We were fortunate, we had just made a payment on the farm before it closed, or we would have been in bad shape.

But we got through it all right, and eventually got ninety percent [of our money] back.

Maud Sloneker, 90, Fayette County

When the banks closed here, my husband had just deposited his first bunch of money in the bank, and then it closed the next morning.

Mary Ash, 84, Shelby County

I can remember the day the banks closed. Dad was a minister, and he had been paid and had put all of the paycheck in the bank except $3.00.

That was kind of a critical time then, because my parents had four small children, and the people in the church who paid him had their problems, too.

I know Dad told them that if they would give him whatever they could spare, why he would stay and make do, because they needed him and he needed them, too.

Margaret Daubenspeck, 57, Rush County

A 1934 Ford at the gas tanks of a small grocery store.
Submitted by Miami County

Did you lose money when the banks closed?

We were starting out, and we didn't have any money to lose.

Mona Winkler, 84, Knox County

I was born of parents that felt that you always should do on what you have, save a little and be independent. Not have to ask anybody for anything, and that has stayed with me all my life.

We had saved—this was in 1932—and we had saved around $800 and some odd cents and we had it in the Grandview Bank. And it was a very, very bitter day when they told us the Grandview Bank had closed, and we had lost all that we had saved from the time we were married. So, we had to start over again.

Eldo Bell, 86, Dubois County

We lost seventy thousand dollars, that my husband had worked hard all his life and made. That was a terrible thing to face. When the bank is gone, your stocks are gone, and everything is gone.

Then he died, not too long after that, and Ruthie wasn't even through school.

And I thought, "What will I do to make a living?" And I thought, "Well, there'll be something." I went down to the Fair Store and I got me a job.

Mary Foltz, 89, Grant County

A friend of my mother's lived over by Kewanna. We went over there one time. She had fell heir to some money, and the Kewanna bank closed, and she lost it.

And that woman, she cried and she went on. She said, "I don't know why I didn't give it to the kids. They could have used it." And she said, "I kept it, and I lost it." That was pitiful.

That was pitiful times and years, I tell you.

Bessie Werner, 80, Pulaski County

What I remember most of the Depression is that he [husband] went to work one morning, and when he come home, he had some money that was scrip. It was worth an amount of money, but we couldn't spend it.

Edna Maddox, 71, Grant County

He first started working in Spencer in 1931. He worked at the stone quarries, as a steam shovel operator.

What was the average pay then?

About forty cents an hour! And at one time they even worked for twenty cents an hour, and they had to take that in what they called scrip as pay, and then they got their real pay later.

Now that scrip, could you buy things with that?

Stores would take it, yes. We could take it to Babbs Grocery Store and get groceries for it.

Was that just good in Spencer, or could you take it anywhere else?
I don't think we could take it anywhere else.
Jane Smith, 78, Owen County

Thinking back about the Great Depression, it was something some of us that have lived through it will never forget. The money that my husband was earning at the Fort Wayne post office was a very small amount, but nevertheless, by dividing it up with our family, we managed to see that everybody had plenty to eat and a place to live.

Frank's brother came back from Kalamazoo, back on the home farm on Amstutz road, completely broke. I remember very distinctly that he would tell that they had ten cents. They had their own eggs, his wife would bake their own bread, and they got along for several weeks with absolutely no money. I think we'd have a hard time getting along with no money now.
Sarah Amstutz, 82, Dekalb County

My parents hung wallpaper during the Depression, and they might work all day and do one or two rooms, and get paid a dollar a room.
Betty Alvey, 60, Howard County

My parents had ten children, six boys and four girls. They lived in Johnson County during the Depression, raising what they ate, and eating what they raised.

Dad had a hired man to help with the chores, and Mom had a hired girl to help with the cooking. When the Depression struck, there was no money for hired help, and the day came when the help was told they would have to go. The money had run out.

This was a sad day for the family, but even sadder for the help. They had no place to go. Tricia was an old maid; there was no financial aid and no family for her to return home to. Slim, the hired man, had no place to go either. They begged to stay, saying they would gladly work for their room and board.

That winter there were sixteen mouths to feed.
Dorothy Dine, 55, Brown County

There is one thing that stands out in my mind. I had a brother-in-law and he and his wife both had good jobs in the shoe factory. He was a foreman, and she was a floor lady.

There was a 120 acre farm, and it was for sale. My mother and I went to visit them, and we tried to get them to sell their stocks and bonds and buy this 120 acres. They said they would think about it, but the farm sold and they didn't [buy it].

Well, when the Depression came, their stocks and bonds just vanished overnight. They had no job, and their money was all gone, because they had it all in stocks and bonds.

So they came here and stayed all during the Depression. They made their home with me from July until February. They had no work, and nothing to eat, and no money to get along on. She helped me can, and they helped us butcher a hog, and we got along just fine.

But they had had the money that they could have paid cash for that farm.

Zada McMillan, 79, Grant County

In 1932, when we were married, Otto was making $9 a week. That was from seven in the morning to six at night, and Wednesday and Saturday nights he was up to the store from four till almost eleven at night.

But we really didn't want for a thing. You could get all the pork chops you could eat for 10¢, a loaf of bread was 5¢, and a quart of milk was 5¢. We just didn't need anything. We had everything we needed with that nine dollars a week.

We also built our own home. My husband had the cement blocks, plaster, sand and gravel, so we didn't need to buy an awful lot for the home. But all the nails, lumber, brick and things we needed to buy the home amounted to $576.40.

Well, then, thirty-six years later we remodeled, and we put two bedrooms upstairs and an open stairway in the living room. It cost quite a bit more than our whole house had cost before.

Florence DeYoung, 68, Jasper County

In 1935, we built our home here, and we have lived here ever since. We paid the laborers twenty cents an hour to build this house. The bricklayers got fifty cents an hour. We built this home for $3,000.

Of course, we did a lot of the work ourselves. My brother hauled the bricks, and I carried them. It was during the Depression and no one had work, so everyone come to help us.

Rosalia Mehringer, 79, Dubois County

CLOTHING

I always wore made-over clothes. I don't think I had a new coat until I was in the 7th or 8th grade. My own new coat. They were always made out of someone else's. I think everyone in my age era can

identify with it. You just used everything you had, and made over.
Evelyn Rigsby, 58, Madison County

Sometimes we would get a package from relatives, with partly-worn shoes and clothes that we always found useful. There was never enough money to buy all the clothes we needed, but we made do by wearing each other's outgrown clothes.
Mable Hunter, 70, Jasper County

We had to do a lot of patching to make the boy's overalls last.
Anna Martin, 79, White County

We always looked forward to going barefooted. We got out of school in April, because we only had eight months of school, and from the last day of school, Sunday was the only day you would put on a pair of shoes.

And you wore them [shoes] out—all the way out—before you got another pair. You had them resoled—Daddy always resoled a lot of our shoes for us—and put new heels on them. You either outgrew them, or else you wore out the uppers so bad they couldn't be fixed, before you got a new pair.
Edna Klinstiver, 57, Floyd County

But you could go down town and buy little dresses for the girls for 30¢, that you would wear anywhere.
Margaret Garrison, 85, Wabash County

I can remember when I bought a dress for a dollar and it wasn't a bad-looking dress at that. A dollar, mind you. And a dollar ninety-eight cents was standard price for dress shoes in Sears catalog.
Florence LaGrange, 81, Perry County

Mother used to make all my clothing. She would take something that someone had outgrown, and then she would redo it for me. So, I had very few brand-new clothes.

It must have been when I was about sixteen, and I needed a coat very badly. We went to the clothing store, and Mother got them to come down to ten dollars on a coat which normally sold for fifteen dollars.

She was going to walk out, and he came to the door and took her offer.
Eleanor Cheek, 61, Union County

How did it affect kids in high school?

Well, for those that were having the hardest time, it was pretty bad, because they couldn't have as nice clothes as some of them that were better off. Of course, we were all pretty much in the same boat, as far as finances were concerned.

People wore very simple clothes—print dresses and at that time we were wearing long cotton stockings. I even started high school still wearing black sateen bloomers, which to me was a great disgrace, but that was all there was.

Thelma Nixon, 67, Union County

I got through high school by having clothes given to me by some neighbor girls who were older than I. Then we always passed our things on to other people.

I remember I was given just a small allotment of money to buy my paper and pencils for school, and I would always try to get along on as little as possible, trying to save a dime or a nickel each week, until I had enough to buy a sweater or something I wanted.

Elizabeth Elbrecht, 60, Dearborn County

I know we wanted special dresses for some party or picnic. Mother said, "You'll have to wear the ones you wore last year," but my dress was too short for me. I was a tall lady. So I gave my dress to my sister, and she had to wear my dress. Mother somehow got another one for me.

Mary Gleason, 77, Perry County

For your high school graduation, your mother did something?

This was still during the Depression. In order for me to graduate, she borrowed $50 on her furniture, which covered all my graduation expenses, except my prom dress, which my aunt bought for me.

What did your prom dress cost? Let's talk about the price of clothing.

I think my prom dress was $7.00.

Was that an expensive dress back then?

Well, medium, but very, very pretty.

Eulalia Slater, 63, Porter County

I had to do all the sewing for the family at that time, ready-made clothing wasn't available much in the stores around, and we didn't have any money to buy it when it was.

But we were fortunate to have the feed sacks in Indiana, and our Indiana feed sacks were among the best in the nation, because they were made with a linen-look weave, and they were printed material.

We had printed material in big prints, little prints and in all colors. We made everything from them.

Was this when you went to the elevator and bought the supplement to add to your own feed? Is that what came in the prints, or how did you get the printed stuff?

We got the chicken feed and the hog feed all ready to feed in it. And at that time you could go to the elevator and buy feed sacks for a nickel apiece. And four feed sacks would make the size of a tablecloth

Perhaps the apron and some of the clothing is made from feed sacks, but the Barber family is happy.
Submitted by Daviess County

or a sheet, and one pillow case could be made from each feed sack.

We made shirts, dresses, men's shirts and all sorts of clothing with them. But this linen-like weave washed; and after it was washed, starched and ironed, it just looked like linen, and it wore well, too. We were fortunate. All states didn't have that kind of feed sacks, but Indiana did.

I made sheets for a lot of people. They would give me their own feed sacks. You could get plain white—for the sheets we used plain white. They would give me their feed sacks and I would sew with felled seams—sew four of them together and make a sheet. And then we talked about it, and word of mouth spread it, and everyone was making feed sack sheets before long.

Didn't it have printing on it?

No, it was plain. You could get plain white.

I thought they had the feed company's name on it, that you had to wash off.

Some of them did and some of them didn't. It depended. I think that was a selling point for some of the feed companies. They found out we wanted them without names on. But if it had lettering on, that lettering wasn't hard to take out, and from then on, it was nice white material.

Did you take whatever you got, or could you choose?

Oh, you could pick and choose.

Did you go choose your own, or did you tell your husband what to get you?

Well, either way. You could go, but usually he did it. But he would see before he went what color I wanted, and if he was getting four sacks, he would get them the same print and the same color. And if he knew that I had some, a couple of one kind, he would look at it and try to match it.

And you made other things out of feed sacks, too?

We made practically everything. And another thing that made lovely table covers at that time was the seed corn sacks. Now it was a little heavier sack, but four of them made a nice square for a square table or a card table. Remember, we put them together with a single tatting or a little crocheting, then around the edge put an edging on to match. And they made beautiful covers.

Virgie Bowers, 81, Pulaski County

Well, us girls [in our Home Economics Club] decided that we'd take these white feed sacks and bleach them out and make pretty dresses. We washed these here feed sacks, and we dyed them all up in the prettiest colors. We had the most pretty colors out on the line you ever saw. There was yellow and pink and green and blue and purple. It took us three or four days to do all that dyeing.

And the patches [scraps], we took what patches there was, and we made comforter tops and we gave them to the poor.

Masa Scheerer, 82, Huntington County

I had a friend that came to stay all night one time. She was used to having the very best. I had my sheets all made out of white mash bags that I had boiled and boiled, because we didn't have bleach.

When she saw those seams, she said, "Oh, my! Can you sleep well on seams like that?" I said, "I sure do, because I work and I am so tired I don't notice a seam."

So, the next morning I said, "Did the seams bother you?" and she wouldn't answer, so I don't know if they really bothered her, or if she didn't want me to know that she had slept all right.

Pearl Sollars, 70, Tippecanoe County

We did lots of things with feed sacks. You know, I still like my feed sack dish clothes better than anything else. Before we left the farm we had lots of feed sacks, and I took about 40 or 50 with me to town. I still have some I haven't worked up.

Once I had some that I thought were especially nice, and I made some curtains for the back room. You tried to make everything do.

There was a challenge to that. You made something out of practically nothing, and it's still a challenge. I like to recycle even to this day. I feel like it is being real thrifty.

Alma Knecht, 78, Wabash County

What was thrown away?
Nothing, nothing! Your knit underwear was cut up into pieces for dishrags, to wash dishes with, and washrags were from that too. You didn't buy turkish toweling washrags.

Dish towels were sugar sacks or feed sacks. The feed sacks were made to use for towels, with a stripe down each side. And I know we had two dishrags—one to wash the white dishes with, but when you got to the kettles you used the black rag. Used it, too, to wipe off your [coal] stove. And when it got completely worn out, you took your white one, and got a new clean white rag to wash the dishes and silver and plates with.

No, nothing was thrown away.

Neva Schlatter, 79, Pulaski County

FOOD

We had an awful hard time a-tryin' to make ends meet. My husband, he'd worked in the quarry and he made 35¢ an hour, and then that run out. And he went to work for a man who came around here gettin' out locust posts. Well, he got a dollar a day for that. We lived on a dollar a day. At that time we had four children.

We moved down there on my grandmother's place late in July, and we didn't have a garden, and my mother's garden had just about give out.

Canning fruits and vegetables was not only necessary, but a source of pride, as well.
Purdue University

And one day I went to look around for something for supper. There was no potatoes, there wasn't anything there. All I had was bacon rinds and flour. I decided I could make biscuits, and that I'd have biscuits and gravy off of it.

And I was standin' out in the back yard wonderin' what I was goin' to do for supper, and my father-in-law drove in, in his old Model T.

And he had a great big flour sack full of cabbage and potatoes and green beans from a late garden.

And I said, the Lord always provides, because he brought all that food for our supper.

Ozetta Sullivan, 73, Harrison County

They always say it is hard to starve a farmer to death.

Olive Wade, Greene County

Well, of course, we lived in the country, and we had a garden and chickens, kept cows part of the time. We just didn't have to buy an awful lot of stuff to get by. That's about all anybody done back during the Depression, was get by.

Alma Smith, 73, Grant County

We sold cream and we sold eggs. We bought coffee and sugar and once in a while cocoa, and, on rare occasions, a can of salmon.

Beulah Mardis, 76, Johnson County

You could buy a box of oatmeal for a nickel at that time, but it was hard to get that nickel.

Pearl Sollars, 70, Tippecanoe County

We never killed a hog, because we thought we could get more by selling it. We would buy bologna, a big piece, and put it in the icebox. I'd make biscuits, and then cut up bologna and brown it in fat lightly and take it out of the skillet and make gravy, then put the bologna in the gravy and have it with the biscuits. Today, I don't like bologna.

Mona Winkler, 85, Knox County

There wasn't much cash to buy anything, but we did have food.

One of my favorite foods during that time was a kind of corn soup. My mother would fix the corn, probably she had canned it, and made it into a milk-type soup, and it was delicious.

I often think, that I should try that again sometime.

Floy Jacobus, 54, Gibson County

My mother and I were talking about the Depression, and, of course, they lived through it. She said we ate a lot of peanut butter and soup beans.

Joan Ford, 49, Jay County

I know we ate a lot of weiners. They were 25¢ a pound, and bread was 10¢ a loaf.

Evelyn Koehler, 68, St. Joseph County

I remember one time we were so low on money, and I needed a loaf of bread. I hunted around until I found eleven cents to buy a loaf of bread. People nowadays, what would they do? They would almost panic, I believe.

Alma Knecht, 78, Wabash County

Hucksters, did you ever know what they were?

No, I'm not familiar with that.

Well, it was a covered wagon. A grocery would have a covered wagon and they'd build shelves and things in there, and they'd put their groceries in there. And these wagons would go through the country.

Like a peddler would?

Yes. And they'd come, I think, once a week. And us kids always liked that, 'cause you'd go out there to that covered wagon. He had a step on the back, and you'd get up on that. Of course, we didn't get in the wagon. He, the man, was in there. You'd tell him whatcha wanted and he'd get it. He had sugar 'n flour, and I think he had some coffee.

He didn't have toys for the kids, then?

No, but he always had candy, and he would give us a piece of candy. We always got up there to get a piece of candy.

They would drive through the summer, till it'd get so cold. In the winter they didn't drive. But we always looked forward to the huckster coming every week.

Was it a horse and buggy?

This was a wagon, and had two horses to it.

Cora Keplinger, 80, Huntington County

The huckster wagon was just a square box-like thing, like a house, and it had lids that come down on each side where you'd put different groceries and stuff.

It was on wheels?

Yes, it was on wheels—pulled by horses. And then in the back was a compartment where he would have gloves and socks and overalls and maybe some yard goods, 'cause he always carried that in the store.

Helen Shockey, 80, Grant County

We had what we called a huckster wagon come by, once a week, and he had all the way from buttons and shoelaces to sugar and lard and all the things, too.

And sewing supplies?

Oh, yes! He had anything you might mention. Probaby even dish pans and things like that. He would come about the middle of the week, and so if you ran out of anything, you could always pick up a few items from him.

Did you pay him cash for these things?

Oh, yes.

Laura Drake, 72, Parke County

In those days the huckster wagon came around to the door each week, and I'd trade eggs and hens for my groceries. Sometimes, if I had a dollar, I might take that out. Do you know, I could go out there with a dollar and come in with almost all I could carry.

Beulah Grinstead, 68, Hamilton County

We got our sugar from the huckster. And you could get two pounds of crackers for a quarter. We generally had enough eggs [to trade for that].

Eunice Houze, 75, Ohio County

We had a bakery truck that came around twice a week, and we bought our bread for 6¢ a loaf from that bakery truck. Then we also had a grocery, a huckster wagon, we called it, that came around once or twice a week, and we would go out and select our groceries from the shelves. We would exchange our eggs for groceries, or if we had some extra chickens that maybe weren't laying. He would have a coop underneath his wagon attached, and we would exchange chickens for our groceries.

Ruth Shrack, 71, Jay County

We didn't have money; the banks had failed and we didn't have a lot of money, but we had a barter system. We would barter products for services. We had a carpenter that we paid in potatoes. My cello was repaired for a ham and a side of bacon. We would trade chickens for things.

It wasn't bad, really. I think it drew the neighborhood together, because we were dependent on each other.

Barter isn't such a bad system.

No, it wasn't. There wasn't a middleman, or sales tax (chuckle).

Blanche Martin, 77, Tippecanoe County

Did your father hire anybody during that time to help on the farm?
He had to hire all the time after my brothers left.

Do you know how much he paid them?
Very little. A lot of it was done by exchange of labor. Us girls would go and help their wives do canning and clean house and things like that. Then they would help us.

Zada McMillan, 79, Grant County

Dorwin went into the business of raising potatoes by the acre. He would take them to Fort Wayne and sell them to the grocers. During the Depression, when he would go to the grocery stores, they would say, "I need your potatoes, but don't have the money to pay for them." Everybody was just so hard up.

Dorwin would say to the grocery keepers, he would say, "That doesn't matter, because I hire a lot of kids to pick up the potatoes and my wife cooks for them." So he said, "I'll take it out in groceries."

He always came back with more groceries that he did money. He would even bring ripe bananas. The kids got to looking forward to the banana deal. When he'd come home, they'd have sliced bananas over homemade ice cream, and that was one thing that the boys looked forward to in meals.

Mary Yerks, 84, Allen County

I was teaching school, and you didn't get much and you had to buy your clothing. But we never paid board at home. Mother never asked us. Well, we worked. We milked, and my job was always throwing down the ensilage at night and helping feed that, so we didn't even offer to pay board.

Hazel Williams, 80, Franklin County

In March we moved to Tipton County, and our salary was to be thirty dollars a month. We got half of the coal we were going to use. We got a gallon of milk a day. We got feed for fifty hens. We got one butcher hog, and our light bill paid.

Beulah Grinstead, 68, Hamilton County

ENTERTAINMENT

What did you do at Christmas time during the Depression?
We just didn't buy. Maybe little things were bought, such as hand-

kerchiefs. People just had to be satisfied. I tried to get things like candy and fruit that the children didn't get very often.

Otillia Buehler, 90, Dubois County

My boys, if they got one new toy for Christmas, they were satisfied. They learned to play with what they had, and to take care of what they had.

Edna Winters, 76, Pulaski County

Mother has mentioned in the last few years that everything we got for Christmas was handmade. I thought it was wonderful, you know. We had the best Christmas presents in the world. For instance, she would take an old doll and put a new wig on it and paint it, make new clothes for it, and it was like a new doll when we got it.

My father made doll house furniture that was out of this world, and small-scale furniture for us to use with our dolls. So we really didn't feel that we were missing anything.

Mary Alice Helms, 45, Franklin County

What went on during Depression days? Where did they go for entertainment?

Well, it was mostly school activities—ball games and class parties. If they could scrape up the money, they took in a show.

Isabel Schoeff, 81, Huntington County

And one time I took my grandma to town to see the doctor. Thurston the Magician was on over in Louisville. And Grandma sit in the car and waited for my sister and me while we went in to see Thurston the Magician. We only had enough money for eating or to go to see him. We decided we could eat when we got home, and, we spent our money goin' to see the magician.

Catherine Summers, 67, Harrison County

During the Depression, I was in high school. We couldn't have anything elaborate, but we had what we called pound parties. Everybody brought a pound of something to the party for food, and that was what we ate for our lunch, for our refreshments.

Maybe you brought a pound of grapes. Grapes then, I think was 10¢ a pound. Or maybe somebody would bring [a pound of] bologna.

We visited at each other's homes then, because we couldn't afford to do anything big. We played what they used to call kissing games. You would spin the bottle, or play post office.

I think we had more parties then than we have today.

Catherine Summers, 67, Harrison County

At that time, we lived in Tipton County. That was a long way from my family and we couldn't go back and forth to visit them. My husband's uncle lived close to us, and that was our recreation then. His wife was a wonderful cook, so we enjoyed going there. We didn't have very much outside activities then, because there wasn't much. If we

During Depression times, families entertained themselves inexpensively at home, as in this 1931 photograph.
J. C. Allen Collection

went to town and went to the grocery, that was as far as the gasoline went.

Thelma Robeson, 73, Fayette County

We were a happy bunch of girls, though, you know. We could just play about any kind of game you know, and after we got older we drove to Sunday School every Sunday. We went to the Methodist

Church and nearly every Sunday afternoon we had a gang of kids at our house—girls and boys. They'd always come to our house.
Mary Wolf, 88, Huntington County

During the Depression, we were fortunate enough that we had work. But some friends of ours didn't have work, and we would have them over for the simplest meals and really I think we had more fun then, because we didn't have to "keep up with the Joneses." Everybody was in the same predicament.
Lucille Greenlee, 75, Marshall County

THOUGHTS ON THE DEPRESSION

There's nine-tenths of the people on welfare today that have got ten times more than I ever had back in my younger days. You got along with what you had, or you done without.
Edna Winters, 76, Pulaski County

We wore out clothes patch upon patch. We prayed much, and believed God would adjust things; and He did.
Clara Nichols, 79, Wabash County

I believe because we were a happy family with a loving mother and father, I survived the Depression years without scars, mentally or physically.
Garnet Parsley, 63, Brown County

The Depression, I think, made us as a family very conservative. We've been that way the rest of our lives. It did something to us. We feel like we can't waste anything—we have to save things and do with less.
Mary Dean, 76, Clinton County

I feel that the Depression did teach us the value of things, and how hard they are to come by. I'm afraid our young people today wouldn't be able to cope with the sort of thing we had to live through back in the 1930s.
Elizabeth Elbrecht, 60, Dearborn County

My mother lived through the Depression. And do you know what my mother's concern was about? That this generation has never learned how to do. They don't save, and they don't use it twice.

Joan Ford, 49, Jay County

What do you think would happen now, if we had a depression?
The first thing, people would just panic, because they couldn't buy what they are used to having. They wouldn't know how to go back and do like we have had to do. I believe it would be pretty bad.

Opal Whitsett, 84, Scott County

I think, if we do have another Depression, I have faith that these young people will learn to adjust, just as I did. I was young, and I didn't know how to do anything, but I learned quick. Kids are just as smart today as they were then.

Ruth Shrack, 71, Jay County

WORLD WAR II

Many women helped the World War II
effort by working in the fields. Since very
few new tractors were built, old tractors
had to be repaired and kept running.
Submitted by Bartholomew County

Do you remember when the war started?

Oh, yes, I remember that real well. I was working here in town and we heard about the war [in Europe] and everybody was talking about it and it was in the newspapers. It was just a great big bore to everybody, 'cause they just didn't think we'd have to go to war.

Masa Scheerer, 82, Huntington County

Do you remember when Pearl Harbor was attacked?

Oh, yes. I remember that was on a Sunday. It was Hugh's birthday. And there were two boys, they always played a lot with Hugh, and they were here that day playing. They had their toys spread out all over the floor when we heard about it.

You heard it on radio?

Yes, on the radio.

Anna Martin, 79, White County

Can you remember Pearl Harbor day?

Yes, I remember it very well. We were at my mother and father-in-laws, and we heard it on the radio. It's the kind of thing you don't grasp the significance of right at first. Then the next day we heard President Roosevelt had declared war, which really set everyone to thinking, when it got to something like that. We just did all the things that we could do to help out.

Thelma Robeson, 72, Fayette County

I can remember very distinctly when they bombed Pearl Harbor and how everybody was so excited, and we knew we were going to be in war. My brother was in the National Guards and he had to go to Mississippi for training right away.

Helen Musselman, 66, Hamilton County

I remember the National Guards being called. We went down from school to see them all off at the train station.

Edna Klinstiver, 57, Floyd County

All the boys were getting drafted. We would go to dances, church, and all the boys in a certain age group were gone. It is an odd feeling to see more girls than boys. When I got out of school, I was working in Evansville, and you would see the boys, but they were all in uniform.

Cledia Bertke, 55, Perry County

I can remember being a senior in high school, and that some of the boys in our class had to go into service before we graduated. It was three or four that didn't go to graduation exercises because they were in service. That made a big impression on us.

Sarah Ziegler, 53, Adams County

How did the second world war affect your life?

A lot! I probably would have been married before I was, if it hadn't been for the war. Bud and I, when we went on our senior trip, we had our first date in Washington, D.C., and then we went together from then on. That was in 1940. Then he left for service in 1942. And the war goes on for two or three years, and you think, "What the heck," so we were married in 1944.

We went to Norfolk, Virginia, after we were married, because he was stationed out there, and we lived near the naval base. We went to the base commissary for all our groceries, and that was our town.

Bud worked on a tugboat for ammunition ships. They reloaded, and Bud said it was about time he was sent overseas. We knew this was coming, but it was just one of the things you didn't talk about. One night he came home thinking it was his last night home and he did leave the next day, but for some reason he didn't go overseas that day.

From then on, for about a week or ten days, when he went to work we never knew whether he would be coming home that night or not. One night, he just didn't come home, and the next day after I waited so long, I went out to the base. I went out to the pier where his ship was (I knew which one it was) and it was gone. It was just that simple.

I sold our furniture to others on the base who were looking for places to live. When one person was done with an apartment, someone else was there to take it. I sold our few sticks of furniture and packed up my little old steamer trunk with what little things I had, and I took my suitcase and a neighbor lady took me to the train station and I came home.

I never felt so alone as when I came home.

My mother-in-law and my mother were waiting for me at the train when I got home, and my mother-in-law said to my mother, "Well, your happiness is my sadness."

I got letters from Bud. Sometimes they'd come all at once, maybe five letters. Then sometimes you'd go six weeks without hearing anything. When you'd get them, they were censored. If there was the least little word in them that they thought might be even a hint of something, that would be cut out. If you wrote on both sides of the paper, it would cut out the back, too. Many times it [letter] was on airmail stationery, because you could get more in the envelope for the weight.

I did not have a star in my window. Many people did. You'd go by a home, and maybe you'd see two or three stars in the window, and it was a reminder.

The European war was over in May, and we thought it can't be too much longer, and everybody was hopeful. When V-J Day came in August I was up at my in-laws at the time. It was my custom to go up and see them one day a week. I would walk up to the corner and catch the bus to Elwood and, as Bud's dad would be on his way home from work, I would ride on up with him. Every Tuesday night I would stay with them and return home the next afternoon on the bus.

That day I had gone down in the car to meet my sister-in-law when she got off work, and the neighbor man down at the end of the lane opened his door and yelled out, "Hey, the war is over."

You could hear horns uptown. We had no televisions, but it was on the radio. What a great feeling! That night I went to Anderson with my sister-in-law and her boy friend, just to see what was going on.

The parade had started down Meridian Street with a constant blowing of horns. You couldn't hardly talk to anybody. I think we were there for two or three hours and they told me it went on all night.

It was that way all over the country. Our church, like many churches, called special prayer meetings in thanks. Just a feeling that you couldn't explain, and it didn't make any difference if the boys weren't home yet. We knew they would be home soon, because it was over.

Bud came home just before Christmas. He called from Chicago. He had come up through Panama and California and from the West. He said, "Hi, I just feel like I'm in the back door right now, and I'm only in Chicago."

Evelyn Rigsby, 58, Madison County

[Editor's note: During World War II, almost every family had near relatives and close friends in the armed services. The interviews are full of stories of sons, husbands, brothers, fathers, uncles and cousins who were drafted or volunteered.

Since many of the narrators have farm backgrounds, they speak of family members who, as farmers, received agricultural exemptions. Other exemptions included the 4-F for physical problems and exemptions for people working in essential industries.

A few quotations, selected from many, follow.]

You know, all my boys were in service, and their father had been in service in the Spanish-American War.

John Grover was in the navy. He was over there in Guadalcanal when they took it. Hubert and Charles and Clyde was in the army. Clyde was in Germany, and Charles was on the Alcan Highway and Hubert was in Italy. Bob didn't get to stay in the service very long. He's always had one bad eye.

You know, I was always whistling and singing, but when the boys were in service, I never sang. Three years I never sang.

You never knew whether they would ever come home or not. You just didn't know what kind of word you'd get the next day. A person don't have no idea how hard it was.

But, thank God, my boys all come home.

Grace Hawkins, 93, Martin County

A World War II young family.
Submitted by Clinton County

I remember that Daddy was worried. He was afraid that if the war kept going, he might have to go, even though he had children.

Men didn't have to go to the war when they had children?

Some men had to go later on, but Daddy was getting older.

Do you remember what age they drafted men?

My husband [to-be] went when he was 17. He was called his senior
year in high school. He had to leave before the senior prom. He did get
his diploma, though.

Wanda Couch, 48, Clark County

Of course, I wondered right away if my husband would have to go
into the service when they started enlisting people. But they didn't take
many farmers, the ones that were established in farming. Some of the
farm boys went, but the ones that were married and had children and
had their own farming operation [were usually exempted].

Was that up to the draft board?

It was up to the draft board of the county. I think each county or
locality.

Thelma Nixon, 67, Union County

Harold's [husband] brother went and he was a prisoner of war for 16
months. Harold didn't have to go. He was 4-F. So he got in at Studebaker as a guard. He was helping the country out, because instead of
fighting, he was making army parts.

Evelyn Koehler, 68, St. Joseph County

Did your father go to war after it was declared?

After Pearl Harbor was hit, he was called. He said he went in for
induction, and he had his pants down, ready to get his shots, and a
man came in and handed him a paper and said, "You're discharged."

Dad said he just pulled up his pants and went out of that room. He
said he never turned around and said good-bye or anything.

Sharon Windhorst, 35, Fayette County

Were any of your sons in WW II?

All three, and all three son-in-laws. We had a flag—one of those
with the stars—we had one in the front window with six stars in it. I
remember a lady passing here one day and said, "I feel sorry for
anyone with six stars in their flag." And I said, "Well, if I was the only
mother with six sons, or any sons, in the service, I might feel sorry for
myself, but I don't. I just trust that they will come back." And they
did.

Iva Crouse, 85, White County

My youngest brother was in it. He was in Austria, and he was still
there fighting three days after the war was over.

He came home very nervous. They kept him there in a hospital for
six to eight months before they let him come home. And when he came

home, he didn't want his wife to sleep in the same room with him, because he was afraid he would hear a noise. They were trained when they heard a noise to be up and ready, and he was afraid if he heard a noise he would hit her or do something to her. It was quite a while before she slept in the room with him.

He got over it finally, with a lot of therapy. He did work in an airplane factory for a while, but the noise was too much. Now he works out in the oil wells in Oklahoma, by himself, and he gets along fine.

Pearl Sollars, 70, Tippecanoe County

We lost a son in World War II. That was pretty trying.

Where was your son killed?

He went down in the Baltic. He was in the air force, and his plane was hit.

What about your other son? Was he too young to go to war?

He didn't have to go, on account of Burdette going down. He wasn't drafted.

Delpha Borradaile, 91, Union County

My husband was in the navy, and I worked in town. You were always concerned. There was always a lot of war movies to go see. And you'd go to the movie and get all worked up, because you could just picture the one you loved being in those places.

Those were sad and trying times for everybody.

Alberta Trout, 57, Grant County

I had two sons that went into the service, and that was pretty rough when you see them leave and go away when you are in war. Peacetime draft is altogether different. It is a different story when you see them leave, and don't know if they are coming back or not.

Emma Baker, 79, Scott County

FOOD

I was teaching during World War II, and it was the rationing I remember most about it. At the beginning of the war, when rationing was first started, school was dismissed for a few days, and the teachers took care of making out the ration cards (or books) for the families in the community. The head of the family came to the school, and the teachers took care of each one of them.

Gasoline, sugar and meat, and I can't remember what else, were

rationed, and each article had its own book that had to be made out.
Ruth Snyder, 83, Marshall County

My most vivid recollection of the 1940s is standin' in line to get everything. I had to stand in line to get meat; I stood in line to get automobile tires; I stood in line to get ration books. I think that was the most vivid part I can remember.
Ozetta Sullivan, 72, Harrison County

Shopping for groceries in World War II was complicated by rationing. Note the sign advertising the OPA ceiling prices and the admonition to have your ration points. The grocer holds a ration book in his hand, and the bread is marked 10¢ ceiling price.
Indiana Historical Society

You had to have stamps for everything during the war. You had to go sign up in an office in your county, and you were issued with these books with stamps which were good for canned goods, for coffee, for meat, even shoes. You had to gauge your living according to your ration books.

It made another job for storekeepers. Besides counting out your change and adding up your bill, they had to add your stamps and how many you owed for that, and then they had to send them in [to the government].

Evelyn Rigsby, 58, Madison County

Since you were in the grocery store, you had to put up with rationing.
Yes, we had to accept those little tokens, those little plastic pieces, about the size of a dime. There were red ones for meat and there was blue ones [for canned goods].

Once in a while, people had extras they would give you, but more often, somebody was wantin' something for nothing.

It was quite a time. I was glad when it was over.

Valetta Ford, 69, Randolph County

I can remember, we traded at a small grocery, and once in a while I would go in to trade, and the old gentleman would come out with a sack with something in it, and he would put that in my basket. He says, "Here is something I think you can use," and it would be soap. Soap powder was very scarce.

Ruth Dye, 75, Martin County

Everyone was allowed a half pound [of sugar] a week, and I don't even use a half pound a week now, but back then people did a lot more baking. They made cakes from scratch; they didn't have box cakes. And they baked cookies. Even if you were going to bake cookies for your son or brother or someone that was in service, you had to take into consideration that you only got so much sugar.

Betty Alvey, 60, Howard County

We'd have to hoard sugar and put it back, so we'd have it when we really wanted it, like for candy making at Christmas time.

Loranelle Kimmerling, 54, Madison County

One of the things I did during this time was to work on a special rationing board. During the summer months, when fruit was in season, people could apply for extra rations of sugar for preserving. I helped fill out these applications.

Kathleen Blondia, 65, St. Joseph County

I remember in our clubs then we had lessons on sugarless cookery.

Thelma Robeson, 72, Fayette County

We learned to bake without sugar. Used to be, you always liked to bake on Saturday, because you wanted cake for Sunday. We got to making a cake with Karo [corn syrup]. We just thought it was great, and it was a fine substitute. The icing was whipped egg whites, and we put Karo in that, too. Saccharin was prevalent, also. It's a wonder we didn't die, because saccharin was used in everything to save sugar.

Evelyn Rigsby, 58, Madison County

When Barbara was small, I needed Karo syrup for her milk, and you just couldn't get that. In fact myself, along with others, would try to be in the store out there at Kingman when they'd get a supply in. They'd open up them boxes, and every woman there would try to grab one of them bottles of Karo syrup, because when that was gone, it was gone. Until maybe two or three weeks, even a month, later.

A World War II ration book for food.
Submitted by Blackford County

This wasn't one of the things that [was rationed]?
No, we didn't have any stamps on it.

Laura Drake, 72, Parke County

What I remember was how sugar was rationed. As a child then, the important part to me was candy and bubble gum. I can remember we lived across the street from the grocery store, and one day a week, the candy truck would come. That would be the only day it would come.

So all the kids would watch for the candy truck and would all go, and there was a long line just to get bubble gum. I can remember standing in that line. I was usually one of the first ones there, because I lived so close and I could see the truck first.

Norma Jean Trent, 47, Dubois County

Each person had a war ration book with stamps, and you could use those stamps to buy sugar or meat. We didn't worry too much about the meat, because we butchered our own, but in cities it was important.

Lois Wagoner, 76, Fulton County

You couldn't get [commercially canned] vegetables unless you had a card, and the card would only allow you so much. We didn't suffer—we had plenty to eat, but we had to be very careful. People in town couldn't put away [can] as much food.

Grace Elrod, 86, Jasper County

I remember, at one time, we had lessons on pressure canning and that must have been during World War II, because it was very hard to buy a pressure cooker, and if you got one, you had to sign, saying that you would allow your neighbors to use it—that you would loan it. It was a form of rationing, I guess. And I got a canner, and I still use it.

Neva Schlatter, 79, Pulaski County

Tell me, what was a victory garden?
A victory garden was a vegetable garden during the war. Everyone was encouraged to raise produce. Our girls took victory gardening in 4-H.

Blanche Martin, 77, Tippecanoe County

In the fifth grade, I was Mary, Mary Quite Contrary in a little playlet that was geared toward World War II. I didn't grow cockle-shells and all that; I grew carrots, beets, potatoes and all those things in my vegetable garden, my victory garden.

Deanna Barricklow, 41, Fayette County

During World War II, Rudolph Leeds, the owner of the *Palladium* [newspaper where husband worked] rented a lot of ground down south of E Street, and anyone who wanted a garden down there could have it.

Horace had a big garden down there. He worked real hard in it. I think there were about 30 gardens down there. One thing I do remember, the *Palladium* used their trucks to go out there and then you'd be there and load the trucks up and they would bring them to you.

It was real hard to find cans, but we finally got cans and did all this canning. I can remember one time everybody stayed home from church and we sat out there in the driveway and fixed lima beans and we had 56 pints of lima beans when we got through. I guess we thought everybody was going to starve to death.

Rudolph Leeds was able to get five pressure cookers, large ones, and the *Palladium* people took turns using those pressure cookers.

Donna Parker, 83, Wayne County

CLOTHING

When we went to the store, they were out of so many things, like at the dry goods stores. I can remember I was short on dresses one Christmas, and my youngest daughter found me enough material to make a dress, and how proud we were of it.

Gladys Tribolet, 71, Huntington County

During the war we learned to live with things; you made do with what you had. You might wear shoes a little longer, because shoes were rationed, and boots were rationed—anything that had rubber in it.

I think about the times when someone died. It was almost like a legacy to get their ration stamps, because they didn't have to turn them back in. Somebody in the family always said, "I'll take their ration stamps to get a pair of shoes," or something.

Betty Alvey, 60, Howard County

Some families used a lot of shoes. We never had too many shoes— we had a dress pair of shoes and everyday shoes. But some of the others had shoes for each outfit, and they needed a lot of shoe stamps. We needed more sugar stamps and gas stamps, so we would trade with each other, so each one would get what they needed.

Ellen McAfee, 68, Marshall County

The American people always rise to a need. We got so we didn't always have to have leather shoes, and we did not need stamps for some of the shoes they had. They didn't last as long, of course, but some of them didn't take as many stamps as others.

Evelyn Rigsby, 58, Madison County

We weren't allowed to wear slacks in school. In fact, I don't think I had a pair of slacks until 15 years ago. We always had to wear skirts

and blouses and sweaters, and we didn't have a great variety of clothes. I remember a pleated skirt and a couple of sweaters that I had.

One time we were in Anderson, and I begged and begged Mother for a sweater that cost $8.00. I remember she and Daddy stood on the corner and had a conference as to whether they'd spend $8.00 for that sweater. I look back now and see that my mother did without something so I could have that sweater, because we all thought that was very expensive.

The Sewing Circle celebrates its first birthday with a cake. Rolling bandages, making comforters and doing other miscellaneous sewing for servicemen (displayed on the comforter) kept these women of all ages busy. Note the pictures on the piano.
Martin Collection
Courtesy Indiana Historical Society

For dress up, it was always hose and girdles, and there was always a "whimsy" veil. I didn't like hats very well, but you wouldn't think of going to church without one, and with gloves and a purse.

I loved high heels. I guess if I had lots of money, I'd have a wardrobe full. I remember the shoe stamps. I had a Number 17 shoe stamp, and I went to town and bought the most gorgeous pair of shoes I think

I ever had in my life, maybe. Blue patent, and at that time you didn't find patent anything except black. They had the heels cut out, sling-back, and no toes. For school it was saddle oxfords.

We occasionally wore hose to school, but rarely, for with the war going on, we just didn't have hose that easily. If we did have them, so many times they were rayon and bagged, or rolled down around your ankles. I guess I've gotten more runs from pulling at them, trying to keep them straight and smooth, but those seams were always crooked.

We had rayon hose, even after the war. I remember standing in line for a pair of nylons.

I was in nurses' training in 1946-47. We still stood in line to get a pair of white nylons. After receiving notification from a downtown store in Indianapolis, girls from various nursing schools and hospitals would all be there the same day, and we'd be lined up for a pair of white nylons.

Loranelle Kimmerling, 54, Madison County

GASOLINE AND AUTOMOTIVE

Gas rationing hit everyone. It really stopped traveling. The farmers got enough to put out their crops, and the ones that worked in town got extra gas, but not enough to do all the things they liked to do. Families would have to get together to go shopping, and things had to be planned to save mileage.

Gladys Tribolet, 71, Huntington County

I can remember you got A, B, or C gasoline ration books, and you had an A, B, or C stamp on your car's windshield.

Valetta Ford, 69, Randolph County

We had one car and he [husband] drove that to work. Gasoline was rationed, but because he was working in the food industry, he was allowed to get the gasoline he needed to go back and forth to work.

Lois Wagoner, 78, Fulton County

On the farm we had to figure exactly how much gasoline it was going to take to do your crops. If you needed extra gasoline for your truck, you had to figure out how many miles you expected to drive.

At that time we were driving a mile and back every day to feed our hogs. We figured up those two miles every day for 30 or 31 days a month, and then figured how many gallons it took. Then you sent it in to the office and they would send you back [the gasoline stamps] you were entitled to.

Betty Alvey, 60, Howard County

Janet was in high school [during WW II], and there was gas rationing. We lived about eight miles from Otterbein, so when there'd be something going on, she—and lots of the country girls—would stay with one of their classmates in Otterbein. She'd stay overnight there, then go to school the next day, and then come home on the school bus.

Helen Weigle, 77, Tippecanoe County

Rationing didn't affect me too much, except for gasoline. At that time my mother was not very well, and I liked to come up to Plymouth to see her at least once a month.

I had been living on the north side [of Indianapolis] and my school was on the south side, and I always drove my car back and forth to school.

I tried to get an apartment on the south side, and finally, after a month of staying in a hotel, I found a little three-room apartment. It was just a mile and a third from the schoolhouse, and I walked that distance all winter long in order to save gas so I could come up home and see my mother once a month.

Ruth Snyder, 83, Marshall County

I was in high school during this period, and there wasn't much socializing, since gas was rationed. They couldn't take school buses to a skating party, or this type of thing, so we really didn't do much. Maybe we went to a show on Saturday night, or some member of your class had a party. During this time I learned to drive a car, and maybe we burned a little more gas than we should have. Many times my father said, "You drove farther than you should have last night."

I think probably we were happier then, because you visited with your neighbors and you did more socializing than we do now. I think that we were more together than we are now, now that we have the money and the gas and every member of the family goes off by themselves in their own direction. At that time, we had to all ride in the same car when we did go.

Floy Jacobus, 53, Gibson County

When World War II came along, we had just went into the automobile business here in Scottsburg. It [war] shut off everything. We couldn't get anything. I spent most of my time in the car, going from one junkyard to another to get parts to fix an automobile.

The men were all working at the Charlestown Powder Plant, and everybody wanted their car fixed at the same time, and you couldn't get new parts to fix them with. That was one of my jobs, to go and hunt up the old parts to fix the cars with.

Zelma Blocher, 81, Scott County

We did without a lot of things. I remember tires were one thing. My uncle died and we tried to go to the funeral, but the tires gave out on us on the way to Cincinnati. We found a man in a garage who was kind enough to fix the old tires. We decided that, instead of going ahead to Cincinnati, we had better turn around and come home, which we did.

Ada Clarkson, 70, Jennings County

Tires were rationed. You could get a certificate for a recapped tire, if you were lucky.

I started to Lafayette one hot day with three kids in the car, and with a hog tied in a metal hog crate on the back bumper of a Model A, and two crates of chickens on the front. I got down on South River Road and blew a tire. I had no certificate to buy a tire. I called my brother-in-law. He came down, and thought it was terrible that my husband would send me to the sale barn with a hog for sale and those chickens, as hot as it was.

Several of the chickens died from the heat. I packed [carried] water and poured over and under that hog to keep it from dying.

The kids were fussing because they were so hot. I always carried some water and a washcloth along when I took them anywhere, so I could wash off their faces and keep them cool.

Ernie finally got a tire he had at home and put it on my car, so I could go on to the sale barn, but the sale was over before I got there.

Did the hog make it home O.K.?

We came back on Monday and took it home. I couldn't take it home that night and take a chance [it might die].

You had a busy day.

One I would like to forget.

Pearl Sollars, 70, Tippecanoe County

EMPLOYMENT DURING THE WAR

And then, during World War II, things picked up and everything seemed to be straightening out a little bit. More jobs were available, and people got on their feet.

Sarah Amstutz, 81, Dekalb County

How did World War II affect your life?

It didn't affect me personally, because I had no one close to me in the service.

But we did everything we could to help our country. We worked hard. We grew foodstuffs so that we could feed the army and really part of the world.

Ada Clarkson, 70, Jennings County

One of the biggest changes in my life was in '41. I got out of high school that spring, and I didn't go to work. I stayed home on the farm and drove the tractor. Daddy had bought a tractor that year, and he did quite a bit of custom baling [using his own equipment and baling hay for hire].

I drove the tractor on the farm, disking and plowing. I was home all the time of an evening when they were working in the fields; we was milking eleven head of cattle then and selling the whole milk to the cheese factory. I was always home to milk the cows and clean up the utensils. I, as a rule, had everything done at the barn when they came in from the field.

I guess that was the only time in Daddy's life he ever done much work on Sunday, but we did custom baling for people on a Sunday, 'cause they couldn't get nobody to bale, and if it looked like rain, we couldn't let the hay spoil. Daddy would go and bale for people out in the Floyds Knobs area, and even up to Sellersburg and down to Corydon. Went quite a distance to help people bale.

Edna Klinstiver, 57, Floyd County

I worked during World War II; I worked at the G.E. (General Electric, Fort Wayne). I was rather smart in arithmetic and I thought I was going to work in an office. And then they told me what they paid in an office, and they told what they paid in a factory. I decided if I was going to have to work, I was going to work in a factory.

So I took the test they had at the G.E. and I went to what they called the G.E. Short School. And I learned to run a lathe like the men run. I learned to read blueprints and all this, and I worked at Winter Street G.E.

When the war was over with, then the men were coming back from the war, and they switched me to a girl's job. I had to take quite a cut in pay . . . *even back then*. But they did give me a little better job, because I had more experience in a lot of things than what a lot of the girls did.

LaVerda Shearer, 56, Whitley County

I worked at Arvin, making ammunition boxes and then I worked in a camp as a cook. I had a job as a PX cook until noon, and then worked in alterations for soldiers and sailors in the evening.

When you worked these places, did you do this with a feeling to help the country?

Everybody worked. Everybody did all they could, it seemed. I don't know why I had two jobs. I could manage two jobs, and I did. I sup-

Working at a factory job during World War II, making parts needed for the war effort.
Bass Photo Collection
Courtesy Indiana Historical Society

pose if there had been more hours in the day, I would have had a third one. It was just the thing to do.

Beulah Mardis, 71, Johnson County

I had a wartime job. The summer between my junior and senior years, I worked in a factory in Anderson, and I had to share a ride, since we were carpooling. A lot of the men had gone to service, and they were using all the girls that they could in factories.

Loranelle Kimmerling, 54, Madison County

Did you have friends who worked in the ammunition factory?

Oh, yes, I did that, too. I helped them make bombshells.

Ellen McAfee, 68, Marshall County

You said you worked as a riveter at the Baldwin Piano Company. What did a piano company make during wartime that was an essential product?

Well, the Baldwin Piano Company was making the ailerons for one of these smaller fighter planes. We made a part of it and I think part of it was made up there at Connersville. Different factories made different parts of the plane. Then they went to one place and they were all assembled there.

Were you checked in and out?

Yes, we were checked. When we would go in or out, they would check to see if we had anything on us. We had guards at the plant all the time, strolling through the plant. We wore badges. My number was 1157.

I think I made 48 cents an hour. They had three shifts part of the time, when they were busy. During the more slack time, there would be only two shifts. I was on the second shift, usually. I would start about three o'clock in the afternoon and work until eleven o'clock at night.

The way you did the work, you drove rivets in with an air gun which resembled an electric drill. You would have an iron bar like a wedge and you would have to hold that up behind the rivet, so it would make it blunt on the other side so it would hold.

Elsie Bossert, 70, Franklin County

When I started to work, everyone wanted to work at those factories, they were making good money.

Marie Unfried, 71, Vanderburgh County

There's another thing I would like to mention about World War II. At that time was when the mothers began working outside of the home so much. We were requested to work in the plants, because so many men were in the war, and they needed us.

It seemed to me, as a teacher, that discipline problems started to become much more prevalent then than they had been before, since the mothers were not in the home.

Ruth Snyder, 83, Marshall County

I believe it started in World War II, the women went to the factories and out into other jobs. They got a taste of being a little bit independent and making their own money.

Then, when the men came home, they didn't want to give up that paycheck, and if their husbands didn't treat them like they thought they wanted to be treated, they had that leverage. "Well, I can take care of myself. I don't need you to support me anymore."

Loranelle Kimmerling, 54, Madison County

It was, I think, during the war years when women started to work away from home, and many of them didn't go back to being just

World War II Red Cross volunteers
roll bandages.
Submitted by Knox County

homemakers after the war. They just kept on with their jobs. They had learned that they could do both jobs. I don't know whether it was a good idea or not, but that's the way the world is now.

Helen Musselman, 66, Hamilton County

HELPING AT HOME

We really didn't have any members of our family in service. They were either too young or too old, or needed in their particular work.

But we took on more work. Tried to produce more. We did everything we could to help.

Blanche Martin, 77, Tippecanoe County

When I was a little girl it was during World War II. Daddy didn't serve in the armed services because he had a heart murmur, and they didn't take him.

But he was a ham radio operator, so his contribution, aside from working on the railroad, was to be a monitor for the different radio bands.

I can recall people coming in and listening with Daddy. They were Red Cross volunteers, and they would relay what they had heard.

So he served his country, even though he didn't serve his country.

We would have air raid [drills] in town, and the whole town would be blacked out. Being only two or three years old, I really didn't understand too much about it, except that the bad guys might be coming, and we had to pull the blinds down and turn all the lights out. I would put my hand over the dial light on his radio, because I was sure the Germans could see that from their airplane.

Deanna Barricklow, 43, Fayette County

I can remember when WWII started, I was terrified. I was five or six years old. I remember I couldn't really grasp what was happening, of course, but I remember sitting at the table and being so frightened, because we'd had blackout drills and air raid drills while we were at school, and we had to go down in the basement and sit down against the wall and all the curtains would be drawn, and it was totally dark. It was terribly frightening, and I can remember being afraid.

I would hear enough of the news to know we were at war, and it was a threat. And Mother would sit down at the table, and she'd say, "Now this is where we live," and a knife would go there, and she would surround us with utensils on the table, just to illustrate that there are people that are going to protect us.

And I remember the stamp sales at school. We took our dimes and quarters. Only I was never rich enough to take quarters, I took dimes. For what did we call them?—our victory stamps? Savings stamps, yes. And I bought my first flute with the bond I had purchased with those stamps. But we took the stamp money every week and bought saving stamps, and that was a great feeling of patriotism, even among the children.

We went out on a beautiful spring day and we all had gunnysacks and we gathered up milkweed pods. They used them, I guess, as kapok or something like that, in life jackets. And the school must have gathered a ton of milkweed pods.

And we gathered paper. My little sister and I—she's three years younger than I—we had a small express wagon. We went around the neighborhood collecting paper which we stored in the garage. My father at that time was driving a truck for a milk company. One Saturday he decided we had enough paper to take down to wherever they took it to turn it in. And when we went to weigh it, we had over a ton of paper. So the newspapers came and took our pictures because we had gathered a ton of paper with our express wagon. And my mother was mortified because we had our old jeans on to have our pictures taken.

I can remember another time, on the Fourth of July. We had Fourth of July celebrations with the neighborhood children in a vacant lot. We were very close to the children in the neighborhood—all of us were—just extremely close. And I can remember dressing up. I think my mother has a picture she took, but we had flags and we wore high-heeled shoes and what we called dress-up clothes. And we went around the block, chanting "General MacArthur, General MacArthur." I have no idea why, but that was our patriotism for the day.

But it did affect all of us, I'm sure.

Mary Alice Helms, 45, Franklin County

It was during the war and they had what they called blackouts. I was a child, but it seems like they were about once a week.

Anyway, this particular night my mom had gone to Eastern Star with our neighbor, Mrs. Dilly, and it was just about time for the blackout to be over. And the neighbor said, "Why don't we go on home. It's almost over with. We can go home without our lights." And there were three ladies sitting in the front seat, and my mother was sitting in the middle. And they had only got about a mile out of town, and they met another person who was also driving without lights. It was the game warden of Greene County. It was right on the curve, and they had a head-on crash.

I'm not sure how this all came about, but they was rushed to the Greene County Hospital. I think it (the crash) was heard, because everything was so quiet during the blackouts. There was absolutely nothing going on. There were no lights of any kind; no businesses were open; no cars on the road; just absolutely quiet. So I suppose this car wreck could be heard for miles.

Our neighbor came to tell us. My Dad was sitting there on the front porch, and it was bedtime for my sister and I, so we were preparing for bed. It was a warm summer night. This neighbor just come to the door and he said, "Francis, Francis, come quick!! Almie's half dead." That's all I remember him saying, 'cause as a ten-year-old child, I was petrified.

But I know we got on our clothes and went to the hospital. My mother laid in that hospital for many, many days with a concussion and many, many stitches on her face.

Mary Ann Hoskins, 49, Grant County

Women of the community organized USO
activities for young men far from home.
Martin Collection
Courtesy Indiana Historical Society

We got married during World War II, and of course everything was rationed. They kept saying when we got married that my husband had always been one of the roughest ones in the shivarees, and that he was really gonna get a ride, so I was scared to death.

My mother-in-law lived with us, and one night we looked out, and here come all these cars down the road with no lights on. We just knew for sure it was the gang coming to shivaree us. I said, "I'm not going to go, 'cause I don't want to take his punishment." So I slipped out the back door. They said, "You won't get far if they're going to shivaree you, 'cause they've got somebody out there to catch you."

I started across the field to the neighbor's house and nobody grabbed me. All those cars kept going on, so I went back to the house and couldn't understand it. We wondered why they didn't stop, and we had to find out. We all piled in our car and followed the cars.

When we got up to them, we noticed there was just one person in each car. We followed them all the way back to town. It was a bunch of women with civil defense, learning to drive in a blackout!!

We never did get shivareed. We didn't know whether to thank the government, gas rationing, or maybe they just give up and it just wasn't worth it.

Betty Alvey, 60, Howard County

One activity of the time was a disaster station set up by the Red Cross. The women of the area gathered there so many times, and we were given instruction on how to set up a food kitchen in case of disaster.

One day, without any notice, we were notified to report. We were tested to see how fast we would gather and put into practice the things we had learned.

You mean the women came just as they were?

Yes, just as they were. One woman who took part said she was cleaning her floors when she was called, and she just dropped everything. She was so embarrassed because her knees were all dirty.

Kathleen Blondia, 65, St. Joseph County

My aunt was a dancing school teacher, so we did a lot of USO work and things like that. I can remember dancing at the gymnasiums and the places being full of soldiers and sailors.

Carol Kobat, 50, LaPorte County

During that time Freeman Field must have kind of run Seymour, didn't it?

That's right. Everybody was connected with the field. Floy Browning and Mrs. Bruce were really pushers as far as the USO and we were always taking groups, or taking cookies to Columbus to Camp Atterbury or down here to Freeman Field, or having parties for the enlisted men.

And there were so many construction people in town then that we were constantly feeding people.

But there were no lasting commitments. I don't think I made a true permanent friend through that whole time, because everybody was transient.

Susie Burkhart, 67, Jackson County

They had a camp down at Camp Atterbury and I was a Gray Lady. They organized a corps of Gray Ladies from Shelbyville, and they asked me to belong to it, and I went down to Camp Atterbury once or twice a week to help.

Were there a lot of soldiers down there?

Oh, yes, I never saw so many pitiful cases in the hospital. They had been in combat, and had come back.

I remember one time we had a picnic for them. They always wanted to go away from the camp, so they took them in buses over to the Brown County Park and some of them went in swimming. There was one boy that we took over there was just wrapped in bandages from his head to feet. He'd been burnt all over. But he was determined that he was going. And when the boys went in swimming, he wanted to go with them, but he couldn't go, of course.

They were just kids, young kids, most of them. That was quite an experience for me.

Camille Hey, 89, Shelby County

War times came along in the 1940s, and my brothers and my one sister went away to service, so that our life was changed by that.

Mother would write letters every Sunday afternoon and Wednesday evening—those were the times she sat down and wrote letters to everyone that was far away.

We would send packages at least once a month, and would write letters more often. We had the V Mail, the victory letters. And they [sister and brothers] always looked forward to letters and packages.

Jean Rechtenbaugh, 52, Marshall County

I felt sorry for all the boys that left Center Point. I still have a big old black bag, out in the garage, with letters in it from different boys. I wrote to everyone from around Center Point and out in the country.

What did you put in the letters?

I tried to give them all the news of Center Point. What people were doing and who had babies and who were married. They seemed to enjoy it, because they would write back and tell me how they enjoyed my letters. I had some fellows send me money [for postage]. That made me feel good, made me really realize that they enjoyed what I was doing for them.

Gaby Moon, 70, Clay County

Ernie [son] was in Germany, in heavy artillery. He got home safe and every once in a while talks about having to ride in those big old heavy trucks.

My mother died while he was in service. I wrote and told him about it, and when he got the letter he was on a big truck just ready to leave on maneuvers. He was just ready to leave, and he read the letter, and he said he couldn't cry then, 'cause there was too much goin' on around, but later on he cried.

He and Mom was awful close.

Edna Maddox, 71, Grant County

The summer I was fifteen, there were no boys around. It was the patriotic duty to write to the boys in service. My neighbor had a brother and she asked me to write to him.

We started corresponding. Two years, and many letters, later we were married on February 21, 1944. I lived with his mother while Morris went overseas, and for the duration of the war.

Dorothy Dine, 54, Brown County

They [sons] were always glad to hear from us and for us to send food. We used to send popcorn, and they would bribe the cooks in the camp to pop it for them.

Iva Crouse, 85, White County

I remember how we—our church women's group—would send packages at Christmas time, send fruitcake and everything. 'Course, I had to be in on that, to help wrap them and package them and address them. That was always a happy time. I mean, it was something that we were glad that we were able to do for them, when they were so far away from home.

Helen Weigle, 77, Tippecanoe County

I was born in '38, so it was going strong when I was little. I had several uncles in the war who served in the infantry.

And I remember, we would take our [sugar] rations and we would make them fudge, big chunks of fudge, and we would send it overseas.

And they loved the treats, their brownies and their candy. They used to write home and say they hardly could get it [package] open, with all the men around them.

And I remember as a child smelling the fudge and helping to pack it, and we really felt like we were helping them.

Sue Cole, 43, Harrison County

I wondered how WW II affected your life.

Well, you see, my kids were gone because of the war. My daughter was working at Indianapolis. She was at the telephone office up there at Camp Atterbury. Raymond was in the service. He was in there 36 months. He was over in Germany 18 months. He never got back until '46.

I tried to help out all I could. I went up with the Red Cross and wrapped bandages, and things like that. I washed for the soldiers over here at George Field, and did that little dab trying to do my part.

It was kind of tough going, but Bill [husband] was over there at the factory and he was working day and night. They had to fill them orders. The soldiers had to eat. That was tough days for everybody, I guess.

Women of the community gather at the local school to bake cookies to pack and send to soldiers in World War II.
Martin Collection
Courtesy Indiana Historical Society

We used to go to George Field. It was a regular city over there. There were thousands of them soldiers over there. They would come to Vincennes and participate in things. I know one time we had a parade and they marched in the parade.

Rita, our daughter, she always got her a boyfriend from over there. Boy, them was the days. She'd write to soldiers. One of them wrote her a letter and said he'd got him a new car—a little red car with white wheels.

One day she was getting ready to go to work and a red car passed our house. I had washed two or three washings and I had them setting in baskets. I said, "Rita, I think that guy's out here." My gosh, she come through here and jumped over all three baskets. She got to the door and said, "Momma, I'm going to kill you." (chuckles) We worked hard, and had a lot of fun.

I remember when they had prisoners of war out here.

Yes, what did they call that park out here (Kimmel Park) by the Wabash River. My husband, Bill, worked over here and he worked them prisoners. So many of them each day, and they would bring a guard with them. Bill said it was hard to work them guys. Nobody could understand them, only the guard.

When they first started out, they'd bring so many men one day, and a different group the next day. Bill was just about to go crazy with that kind of doings, so he told his superintendent that he was going to quit if they didn't send the same men every day. So they did that.

There was an awful bunch out there. We used to go out there and watch them. They had a fence all around it. They said it was just like Germany inside, they gave them all the beer they could drink. They ate pretty good here, too, I think.

Like I said to one of the guards out there, "Ain't it pitiful?" And he said, "Pitiful? If it wouldn't be for them guys, I wouldn't have to be here!" And that's right, you know. Here we was standing there, feeling sorry for them, and they was the cause of it.

Hazel Dolkey, 79, Knox County

After World War II came along, everybody had more money than they used to have. They got better prices for corn—corn went up to a dollar a bushel.

We lived just like we had been living, conservatively, and working hard and putting our stuff to use. But some went wild spending money. They paid $20 for a shirt, and I don't know how much for shoes, just because they had it to spend.

Grace Elrod, 86, Jasper County

END OF WAR

And I remember the northern lights came into the sky. It was the most unusual thing we had ever seen. We thought it was a sign from God. Right in the center was an eagle. I remember us all laying on the ground, and we watched that sky. It was the most frightening thing I had ever seen.

And you thought it was the end of the world?

No, we really felt it was a signal that things would come out all right. That maybe the U.S. would win. It sort of gave you confidence and hope.

Libby McKinney, 53, Bartholomew County

I remember the day when President Franklin Roosevelt died. My mother sent me up to where all the men were working, to tell them. I didn't even hardly know who Franklin Roosevelt was, but I thought it must be pretty important. I remember going up and telling them.

Carol Schroeder, 45, White County

I think, in history, the first that I remember was when Roosevelt died. The radio and everyone, that was something that people really took notice of. I remember people sitting around crying. It really did get everyone's attention. It wasn't just a passing thing.

Juanita Harden, 49, Bartholomew County

When the war was over, that was a holiday for everybody. Everybody went a-whooping and a-hollering uptown, and we heard it at 1:00 at night. So we got up and we went downtown to see what was going on; to find out why the bells and the whistles and everything was a-blowin' like crazy. My girlfriend and I, we walked down to find what it was. They said, "Oh, the war is over." Well, everybody was happy! They was dancing in the streets and a lot of them was just a-crying and carrying on, they was so tickled.

Masa Scheerer, 82, Huntington County

I remember when the war was over, everyone went to town and drove and drove and had a big parade and [were] waving flags and hollering. Some people were crying. It was quite an experience to think it was finally over and the boys would be coming home.

Betty Alvey, 60, Howard County

[County sheriff's wife speaking] We were there when the war was over. Bud directed traffic. And it poured rain and people just rode and blew their horns and celebrated all night, nearly.

Did people come in from the country, too?

Yes, they came to celebrate.

Everybody had somebody in the war, almost, and it meant a lot to everybody. We thought everything was just going to be perfect, from then on.

Kathryn Grinstead, 71, Rush County

Many people who went through the war didn't really think of it as a sacrifice at the time, because everybody had the same thing in mind. I think we are very aware of the many privileges we have.

Evelyn Rigsby, 58, Madison County

FIFTIES, SIXTIES
AND SEVENTIES

Young people enjoying the post-World
War II period. Note 1949 license plate on
car, the bobby socks and the saddle shoes,
and the longer length skirts of the
New Look fashion.
Submitted by Dubois County

When the war [World War II] was over, that was a big time for us in business. They began to make automobiles and you'd just get one once in a great while, and you had a long list of names of people waiting for them. You would get one car, and everybody that was on the list would come and see if their name was there. So that was a hard time, too, but it was all enjoyable.

I remember, after the war was over and we began to get new cars in, we were selling Studebaker cars, and the first new one was different from anything that we'd had. I drove the car one afternoon to Madison to buy parts.

New post-World War II Hudson
automobiles, at an agency which bills itself
as the "Largest Hudson Dealer
in the Country."
Martin Collection
Courtesy Indiana Historical Society

No one had seen the new cars yet and when I came out of the parts house, there was so many people around it. Some of them were even down on the ground, looking under it. I didn't know whether I was ever going to get home with it or not, because every stop I made, people came out to look at the new car. And they were more anxious than ever to get one as soon as they came in.

We had a lot of difficulties and problems satisfying people, because everybody wanted a car at the same time. We didn't get very many, because they were so slow about coming in. We'd had things built-over for so long that we wanted something new.

Zelma Blocher, 81, Scott County

My son wasn't in World War II, he was in the Merchant Marine at that time, but he was in the Korean War. He was in a year and a half. He was in that Chosen Reservoir where they were surrounded in North Korea.

What were some of the things you might send to help the servicemen?

When Don went, he wrote a letter that he was going into North Korea, and he said he expected it would be the last letter we'd get from him.

Well, he loved popcorn, so we got a can of popcorn and some oil and fixed up some of the things he liked. When he got out of the Chosen Reservoir and got back in South Korea, the boys laughed at him and said, "So now you've got popcorn, what are you going to do with it?"

He told them not to worry, that his mother would have something in there. He took off his helmet and washed it out and there was the oil. He built a fire and put the oil in his helmet, and they had popcorn popping all over the camp.

Juanita Hunter, 81, Scott County

My husband was in the Korean War, in fact he was wounded rather seriously in Korea. He lost his eyesight, but was fortunate enough to have a good surgeon who restored it over there.

I can hear a great deal of bitterness when he talks about some of the rioting against being drafted. Anyone who isn't willing to serve his country, he's very bitter about it. I hear that when he's talking to the kids, too.

Of course, I don't want Scott to ever have to go to war, or the girls either, and I'm sure he doesn't either. But there's a strong feeling that, if that comes about—if that is what happens, then it's his duty to go.

Mary Alice Helms, 45, Franklin County

One of your sons was in the war?

Well, he went in 1954. 1955 was when he was killed. It was past the Korean War; it was over. But they drafted them anyhow, at that time. He enlisted because he knew he'd be drafted, and he went into the Air Force.

Ozetta Sullivan, 72, Harrison County

Can you remember anything particular in the '50s?

In the '50s my daughter graduated from high school, and I

remember more of her activities than my activities—I was just busy teaching school. But they had lots of dances, and it just seemed to me that every dance, it was, "Mom, I have to have a new skirt." And the making of pom-poms, and the craze for boys. This was all in the '50s.

Lucille Greenlee, 75, Marshall County

Let me think back to the '50s. That was when I was growing up, and I remember it as a prosperous time. My family did a lot of things. We always seemed to have enough.

Rebecca Stewart, 35, Franklin County

My dad was a ham radio operator.

When I was a senior in high school, in '57, Daddy came downstairs and he said, "I want you to come upstairs and listen to this." So Mother and I went up and listened in his room, and there was this strange little peep, peep, peep.

He said, "I don't know what that is, but it's something different, and we're going to hear about it." Well, it wasn't a week that the Russians announced they'd sent up the satellite Sputnik, and Daddy had gotten this signal on his radio.

And then in later years, after I was married, Dad was talking to a missionary from our church who was in Africa. His name was Hale Whitcomb, he was a Connersville boy. And Hale said, "Joe, I've got to go; we're going to have to get out of here."

Dad didn't turn off the radio and he could hear gunshots. Terrorists had come into the courtyard of their area there. They weren't after the missionaries, they were after someone else. He [Dad] called a fellow in Richmond who had a contact with someone in Africa who had an airplane. And because of Daddy's accidentally hearing Hale, he was able to indirectly help get that airplane to them at a certain point, after they had ridden belly-down in a canoe on a river. They met them at an airstrip and they were able to flee, with bullets going over them.

Deanna Barricklow, 43, Fayette County

In the '60s, I didn't see much change early on. I was in school in 1964. I remember the civil rights bill going through Congress. Of course, it didn't affect us much in Franklin County, but I was in school in Lexington, Kentucky, and I can remember people talking about it. And I can remember thinking, "I'm amazed that they didn't think of that sooner. Why has it taken so long to get to this point?"

It wasn't really until the '70s when we had all the disenchantment with the war, and I can't say that really affected me. There was a lot of unrest on the college campuses, but it was before this that I had attended school. But I've read a little bit about it.

Your age group was the one that was involved in the Vietnam War. It was all right for our age group to say, "Okay, you are going to go," but it wasn't our age group that went. It was your age group that was taken.

Yes, and at that time I did not question it. I accepted the Establishment's idea that that was the thing to do.

It didn't cause a confusion over "This is what I think I should do, but this is not the right thing to do?"

Oh, no. But these things are so difficult—it's hard to know what is right. And, after I've read a little bit about it, I wonder if it was right.

But I really can't say that the Vietnam conflict changed my life in any way. Now my husband, healthy as he is, he was classified 4-F, which I always thought was amusing, but I was thankful.

Rebecca Stewart, 35, Franklin County

Donald [husband] enlisted in the Marines for four years and that was when the Vietnam War was going on. He only spent three or four months in Vietnam because he was injured. He and another guy were out on patrol. They were ambushed by the Viet Cong and shrapnel from a hand grenade blinded him in one eye. The other boy that was with him was killed.

He still has a lot of thoughts and dreams about Vietnam. He was a radioman and radiomen had to be particularly on guard because the antennaes they carried on their backs stuck way up and lots of times that is how they spotted the guys that were out on patrol.

He doesn't have too many pleasant thoughts about Vietnam. He does feel that Vietnam veterans were short-handed when they came home and are now. He feels that they owe them just as much honor as they do other guys that maybe went to World War I or World War II.

Because they were just doing their duty to go over there and fight, and so many guys that went over there died.

Bobby Henry, 30, Union County

Would you tell us about the experience you had when your son was a prisoner of war?

Well, he was captured September 16, 1966, and he wasn't released until March, 1973, so he was a prisoner for six and a half years.

They sent a telegram that he was missing in action, and that was brought by someone in the service. We were fortunate, because the serviceman got kind of mixed up on the streets, and he went to the Christian Church parsonage.

Harold Barnett is a special friend, and he just knew when he opened the door that it was something serious, so he invited him in and found out what his mission was. Then he called Jim and had him come over. Then they came down here and told us. It made it easier that way, than if some of us would have gone to the door and seen this fellow there by himself.

Was he being held by the Vietnamese?

Yes, he was in North Vietnam. The next month, in October, Ray Mano was listening to the radio real early, and he heard a broadcast from Japan about prisoners being taken, but he just got the tail end of the names. So we investigated that, because we figured it was Hubert, and it was. So we knew that soon that he was still alive. The Air Force didn't notify us until December, officially, that he was a prisoner, but we had known it since October.

Did you know whether your letters and packages were getting to him or not?

No. I think I received about twenty-five letters from him all the six and a half years he was gone. The first package that I fixed and mailed to him was returned, and I didn't open that for a year. I just couldn't.

Evelyn Buchanan, 78, Scott County

THOUGHTS ON WAR

In World War I, I had brothers that went, and one of my brothers never came home. He went down in the English Channel.

Then, [in World War II] when my oldest son was 18, he was drafted, and he signed up for the navy.

My second son was called up then, but the day they were to leave, they sent him home with a 4-F exemption. So he came back home and married and started farming. Later on they called him, and he was sent to Korea. He had to help guard the line between North and South Korea.

Then I had a nephew that fought in Vietnam and he stepped on a mine and it killed him.

So, I went through several wars, but you have to take the mental attitude on it that somebody has to protect us. Somebody has to go. My husband, brothers, children and nephews have all gone. I haven't had a grandson yet to go, but I might have to. I sure would hate to see that, but we just have to defend our country and take things as they come, and trust in God that things will work out.

Ruth Dane, 81, Madison County

*"And isn't it a God's blessing
if you'd never have no more
wars. I hate wars."*

Masa Scheerer, 82,
Huntington County

ACKNOWLEDGMENTS

With a statewide project of this size, almost completely done through volunteer work, no list of acknowledgments could possibly include the name of everyone who has contributed. Most of the membership of the Indiana Extension Homemakers Association has contributed in some way, if not by active participation, at least by enthusiasm and support.

The volunteer interviewers conducted the fine interviews which are the basis of the whole project. Many of them, in addition, transcribed the interview they had made, spending many additional hours in the process. Their contribution is incalculable.

Equally to be thanked are the narrators, the people who talked to our interviewers, sharing with us their experiences, memories and values. They have offered us their finest compliment, their trust, as they shared their lives with us.

Because of space limitations, this book can contain only a small portion of the fine material contained in the interviews. Every interview has been read and studied many times. All are extremely useful for background and research, both in this project and for future historians.

The list which concludes this section contains the names of narrator first, interviewer second, listed by county in alphabetical order. Without these people, there would have been no project.

Thanks go also to the women who shared their photographs and other visual materials with us. Their contributions, too, were vital to the project.

Chief consultant to the project from the beginning has been F. Gerald Handfield, Assistant Director of Field Services, Indiana Historical Society. The project owes much of its depth and scope and all of its oral history expertise to his knowledge, enthusiasm and energy.

Other consultants who have shared their insights have been D'Ann Campbell, Dean of Women's Affairs, Indiana University; Alice Shrock, Department of History, Earlham College; and Cullom Davis, Department of History, Sangamon State University, Illinois.

Paul Wilson, photographer and producer, traveled many miles in recording the visual material. His professional expertise and unfailing good humor and dependability have been much appreciated.

The Oral History Committee of the IEHA has given advice, inspiration and hard work to the project. They have indexed interviews and sorted excerpts to make a large body of information more accessible to all. Current members are: Coleen Allmandinger, Betty Alvey, Dorothy Anderson, Julia Binkley, Margaret McClain and Nancy Prue. Former members include Annette Hitch and Bettie MacMorran. Betty Alvey has spent many extra hours mailing book orders and the slide/tape program. Coleen Allmandinger coordinated publicity for the project, including editing the brochures for the books and slide/tape program. Margaret Boilanger has kept perfect financial records for the project. The members of the Board of Directors of the IEHA have been supportive in all ways, as have been the home economics agents in each county and the staff at Purdue, particularly Ann Hancook, IEHA advisor.

Thanks are due the Indiana Committee for the Humanities for past financial support to the Indiana Historical Society for making its personnel, facilities and files available and for agreeing to serve as final repository for materials from the project.

Purdue University, Indiana University, and the Indiana State Library have served as cooperating institutions, sharing their personnel and facilities.

David Stahl has served as graphics director for the books.

A final word of thanks goes to the editor's long-suffering family who have been so interested and supportive in every way. Little Grace, my six-month-old granddaughter, has served as part-time co-editor from her baby seat in my office, and my husband has supported me fully and encouraged me always.

LIST OF SOURCES

INTERVIEWEE, *INTERVIEWER*

FULTON COUNTY
Trella Feidner, *Doris Hill*
Pearl Hiland, *Shirley Willard*
Irene Rouch, *Doris Hill*
Lois Wagoner, *Shirley Willard*

GIBSON COUNTY
Floy Jacobus, *Ruby Rumble*
Essie Rumble, *Ruby Rumble*
Beatrice Shuel, *Ruby Rumble*

GRANT COUNTY
Berniece Corey, *Zada McMillan*
Mary Foltz, *Lauretta Brock*
Mary Ann Hoskins, *Marjorie McDonough*
Icil Hughes, *Marjorie McDonough*
Zada McMillan, *Lauretta Brock*
Edna Maddox, *Marjorie McDonough*
Helen Shockey, *Lauretta Brock*
Alberta Trout, *Zada McMillan*
Alma Smith, *Marjorie McDonough*

GREENE COUNTY
Lula Hasler, *Mildred Duzan*
Blanche Heaton, *Olive Wade*
Anna Workman, *Olive Wade*

HAMILTON COUNTY
Agnes Bell, *Wanetta Edgerly*
Alice Gentry, *Naomi Williamson*
Beulah Grinstead, *Wanetta Edgerly*
Grace Heinzman, *Sandra Wire*
Helen Musselman, *Wanetta Edgerly*
Beulah Rawlings, *Sandra Wire*

HANCOCK COUNTY
Helen Rushton, *JoEllyn Kennedy*
Mary White, *Louise Garrett*

HARRISON COUNTY
Leora Haub, *Elaine Crawford*
Maude Faith, *Diana Kirk*
Ola Kintner, *Ruth Rosenbarger*
Sue Cole, *Elaine Crawford*
Catherine Summers, *Elaine Crawford*
Ozetta Sullivan, *Elaine Crawford*

HENDRICKS COUNTY
Flossie Foster, *Dorothy Kelley*
Leona Hunt, *Mary Moore*
Dorothy Kelley, *Mary Moore*
Mary Moore, *Dorothy Kelley*
Mildred Newby, *Mary Moore*

HENRY COUNTY
Dora Mattox, *Cordelia Wright*
Cheryl Moore, *Cordelia Wright*

HOWARD COUNTY
Betty Alvey, *Rose Russell*
Edna Vandenbark, *Betty Closson*

INTERVIEWEE, *INTERVIEWER*

HUNTINGTON COUNTY
Cora Keplinger, *Pat Fitch*
Masa Scheerer, *Mona Harley*
Isabel Schoeff, *Pat Fitch*
Gladys Tribolet, *Mona Harley*
Mary Wolf, *Pat Fitch*

JACKSON COUNTY
Susie Burkhart, *Judith Wichman*
Hilda Thomas, *Judith Wichman*

JASPER COUNTY
Opal Amsler, *Sharon Schulenberg*
Florence DeYong, *Laverne Terpstra*
Grace Elrod, *Rachel Tulera*
Mabel Hunter, *Laverne Terpstra*
Inez Walther, *Laverne Terpstra*

JAY COUNTY
Joan Ford, *Gladys Houser*
Thelma Reedy, *Gladys Houser*
Thelora Shoemaker, *Gladys Houser*
Ruth Shrack, *Gladys Houser*

JENNINGS COUNTY
Ada Clarkson, *Mary Bowman*
Lillian Gookins, *Jacqueline Nentrup*

JOHNSON COUNTY
Elsie Canary, *Carol Spurgeon*
Beulah Mardis, *Carol Spurgeon*

KNOX COUNTY
Hazel Dolkey, *Grace Kocher*
Mara Meyer, *Grace Kocher*
Mona Winkler, *Grace Kocher*

LAKE COUNTY
Nellie Depew, *Eleanor Arnold*

LAPORTE COUNTY
Beverly Barnes, *Marilynn Livinghouse*
Florence Carson, *Marilynn Livinghouse*
Carol Kobat, *Marilynn Livinghouse*
Karren Saboski, *Sherry Deutscher*

LAWRENCE COUNTY
Eula Kelso, *Phyllis Westfall*
Vida Mundy, *Phyllis Westfall*
Mary Sheeks, *Phyllis Westfall*

MADISON COUNTY
Ruth Dane, *Kay Kinnaman*
Loranelle Kimmerling, *Kay Kinnaman*
Elma Matthew, *Judy Smith*
Evelyn Rigsby, *Kay Kinnaman*

MARION COUNTY
Beulah Thompson, *Jerry Handfield*

INTERVIEWEE, *INTERVIEWER*

MARSHALL COUNTY
Lulu Graves, *Jean Rectenbaugh*
Lucille Greenlee, *Jean Rectenbaugh*
Isabella Johnson, *Jean Rectenbaugh*
Jean Rectenbaugh, *Jean Rectenbaugh*
Frances Harley, *Lucille Greenlee*
Mary Hawkinson, *Jean Rectenbaugh*
Ada Hutchings, *Jean Rectenbaugh*
Ellen McAfee, *Lucille Greenlee*
Helen Samuelson, *Jean Rectenbaugh*
Ruth Snyder, *Jean Rectenbaugh*

MARTIN COUNTY
Cleo Borders, *Ina Baker*
Ruth Dye, *Ina Baker*
Dorothy Fuhrman, *Carla Hoffman*
Grace Hawkins, *Carla Hoffman*

MIAMI COUNTY
Donna Agness, *Margaret McClain*
Chloe Golden, *Margaret McClain*

MONROE COUNTY
Edith Lawson, *Mabel Mood*
Emily McConnel, *Mabel Mood*
Muriel Voliva, *Mabel Mood*

MONTGOMERY COUNTY
Ethel Downed, *Dee Ann Cabell*
Juliana Huseman, *Dee Ann Cabell*

NEWTON COUNTY
Hi Neighbors, *Janet Boston*

NOBLE COUNTY
Della Ackerman, *Jeanette Jacob*
Opal Becker, *Jeanette Jacob*
Dorothy Raub, *Jeanette Jacob*
Lucile Imes, *Jeanette Jacob*

OHIO COUNTY
Clara Ashcraft, *Hazel Sullender*
Eunice Houze, *Hazel Sullender &
Betty Taylor*

OWEN COUNTY
Pearl Kincaid, *Mary Weilhamer*
Jane White, *Mary Weilhamer*

PARKE COUNTY
Stella Irwin, *Ellen Lang*
Hazel Thomas, *Priscilla O'Haver*
Clyde Smith, *Ellen Lang*
Theresa Bramblett, *Priscilla O'Haver*
Myrtle Fisher, *Ellen Lang*
Laura Drake, *Priscilla O'Haver*

PERRY COUNTY
Rosemary Flamion, *Nellie Frakes*
Nellie Frakes, *Nellie Frakes*
Mary Gleeson, *Nellie Frakes*
Florence LaGrange, *Marie Lynch*
Cledia Bertke, *Becky Blum*

INTERVIEWEE, *INTERVIEWER*

PIKE COUNTY
Marjorie Malott, *Marjorie Malott*
Colista Rogers, *Marjorie Malott*

PORTER COUNTY
Margaret Larson
Elsie Nickel
Eulalia Slater, *Claudia Slater*
Dolores Slater, *Claudia Slater*
Inez Smith, *Marian Smith*

POSEY COUNTY
Audrey Blackburn, *Sharon Sorenson
& Judy Knowles*
Theresa McFadin, *Sharon Sorenson
& Judy Knowles*
Vernell Saltzman, *Sharon Sorenson
& Judy Knowles*
Thelma Roehr, *Sharon Sorenson*

PULASKI COUNTY
Virgie Bowers, *Julia Binkley*
Neva Schlatter, *Julia Binkley*
Mildred Weaver, *Julia Binkley*
Bessie Werner, *Julia Binkley*
Edna Winter, *Julia Binkley*

PUTNAM COUNTY
Marian Job, *Mary Sharp*
Elizabeth McCullough, *Mary Glidewell*

RANDOLPH COUNTY
Valetta Ford, *Helen Symonds*

RIPLEY COUNTY
Ethel Meyer, *Ruth Huneke*
Pearl Snider, *Ruth Huneke*

RUSH COUNTY
Margaret Daubenspeck, *Juanita Rees*
Theresa Fecher, *Juanita Rees*
Kathryn Grinstead, *Eleanor Arnold*
Shirley Morgan, *Virginia Wright*
Marie Weber, *Virginia Wright*

SCOTT COUNTY
Emma Baker, *Doris Prewitt*
Zelma Blocher, *Doris Prewitt &
Delia Everhart*
Evelyn Buchanan, *Doris Prewitt*
Margaret Dean, *Doris Prewitt*
Opal Whitsett & Juanita Hunter,
Doris Prewitt & Delia Everhart

SHELBY COUNTY
Mary Ash, *Jewel Luhring*
Mabel Bobbitt, *Jewel Luhring*
Thelma Fox, *Jewel Luhring*
Opal Gallagher, *Jewel Luhring*
Camille Hey, *Eleanor Arnold*

SPENCER COUNTY
Eldo Minor Bell, *Helen Kennedy*

INTERVIEWEE, *INTERVIEWER*

ST. JOSEPH COUNTY
Kathleen Blondia, *Inez Reum*
Helen Marker, *Inez Reum*
Joyce Frederick, *Norma Cline*
Evelyn Koehler, *Norma Cline*
Burnetha Knox, *Norma Cline*

SWITZERLAND COUNTY
Mildred Cochran, *Rachel Hickman*

STEUBEN COUNTY
Margaret Butler, *Virginia Hill*

TIPPECANOE COUNTY
Blanche Martin, *Martha Cox*
Mildred McCay, *Julia Binkley*
Pearl Sollars, *Martha Cox*
Helen Weigle, *Katherine Delaney*

TIPTON COUNTY
Clara Carter, *Elizabeth Barton*

UNION COUNTY
Delpha Borradaile, *Susan McCormick*
Eleanor Cheek, *Susan McCormick*
Bobby Henry, *Susan McCormick*
Thelma Nixon, *Susan McCormick*
Gleda Stevens, *Susan McCormick*

VANDERBURGH COUNTY
Lulu Rheinhardt, *Mary Herron*
Nancy Schneider, *Lois Appel*
Marie Unfried, *Lois Appel &*
  Mary Herron
Edna Vandenbark, *Lois Appel*

VERMILLION COUNTY
Trilla Alderson, *Marguerite Albright*
Florence Miller, *Marguerite Albright*

INTERVIEWEE, *INTERVIEWER*

VIGO COUNTY
Mable DeWitt, *Marjorie Bedwell*
Beulah Fessant, *Joan Cox*
Thelma Shelburn, *Joan Cox*
Clara Stuthard, *Joan Cox*

WABASH COUNTY
Margaret Garrison, *Louise Dawson*
Alice Guyer, *Louise Dawson*
Mary Johnson, *Louise Dawson*
Alma Knecht, *Louise Dawson*
Clara Nichols, *Louise Dawson*

WASHINGTON COUNTY
Lulie Davis, *Bonnie Pruett*

WAYNE COUNTY
Mary Graver, *Mary Mathews*
Mary Mitchell, *Shirley Wise*
Donna Parker, *Mary Mathews*
Helen Sauser, *Mary Mathews*
Jackie Webb, *Shirley Wise*

WHITE COUNTY
Iva Crouse, *Carol Schroeder*
Anna Martin, *Carol Schroeder*
Alene McKinley, *Carol Schroeder*
Doris Stevenson, *Nancy Prue*
Alfreda Wesner, *Carol Schroeder*

WHITLEY COUNTY
Ruby Leedy, *Helen Murbach*
Maggie Owen, *Helen Murbach*
LaVerda Shearer, *Helen Murbach*

Gary ●

South Bend ●

LAPORTE ST. JOSEPH ELKHART LAGRANGE STEUBEN

LAKE PORTER

NOBLE DEKALB

MARSHALL

KOSCIUSKO

STARKE

WHITLEY ALLEN

NEWTON JASPER

PULASKI FULTON

● Fort Wayne

WABASH HUNTING-
TON

WHITE CASS MIAMI

WELLS ADAMS

BENTON

CARROLL

GRANT

TIPPE-
CANOE

HOWARD

BLACK-
FORD JAY

WARREN

CLINTON

TIPTON

MADISON DELAWARE

Lafayette ●

MONT-
GOMERY BOONE

HAMILTON

Muncie ●

RANDOLPH

FOUNTAIN

HENRY

PARKE

WAYNE

HENDRICKS MARION HANCOCK

PUTNAM

Indianapolis ●

RUSH

VERMILLION

SHELBY

FAYETTE UNION

VIGO CLAY

MORGAN JOHNSON

FRANKLIN

Terre Haute ●

OWEN

DECATUR

MONROE BROWN BARTHO-
LOMEW

DEAR-
BORN

SULLIVAN

RIPLEY

GREENE

● Columbus

Bloomington ●

JENNINGS

JACKSON

OHIO

LAWRENCE

KNOX MARTIN

JEFFERSON SWITZERLAND

DAVIESS

WASHINGTON SCOTT

Madison ●

ORANGE

CLARK

PIKE DUBOIS

GIBSON

CRAWFORD HARRI-
SON FLOYD

POSEY VANDER-
BURGH WARRICK PERRY

SPENCER

● Evansville

INDIANA HISTORICAL BUREAU
140 North Senate Avenue
Indianapolis, Indiana

COLOPHON

This book was typeset by photocomposition in
the Times Roman series of type. This typeface
was originally designed to be used in the news
columns of the *London Times*. Because of its
attractive appearance and readability it has
become one of the most popular text faces
used in books today.

Book series designed by David Stahl
Typography and printing by Metropolitan Printing Service, Inc.